PENGUIN CLASSICS

THE UPANISHADS

ADVISORY EDITOR: BETTY RADICE

JUAN MASCARÓ was born in Majorca. The beauty of the island, then unspoilt, and the strength of the living folk tradition made a deep impression on him as a child. At the age of thirteen he copied a book on occultism, but this proved spiritually misleading. However, he found a reading of the *Bhagavad Gita* highly illuminating, although it was in a poor translation, and this led him to learn the elements of Sanskrit. Later he went to Cambridge, where he read modern and oriental languages, Sanskrit, Pali and English.

He lectured in Oxford on the Spanish mystics, and then went to Ceylon, where he was Vice-Principal of Parameshvara College at Jaffna, and to the University of Barcelona, where he was Professor of English. After the Spanish Civil War he settled permanently in England. He lived at first on the hills above Tintern Abbey; he translated some *Upanishads* and the *Bhagavad Gita* (also a Penguin Classic). He then returned to Cambridge University, where he was a supervisor in English and lectured on 'Literary and Spiritual Values in the Authorized Version of the Bible'. He also translated the *Dhammapada* from Pali for the Penguin Classics. He married Miss Kathleen Ellis in 1951 and they had a son and daughter. Juan Mascaró died in 1987. *The Times* obituary described him as a man who had 'achieved the unique feat of translation from languages not his own (Sanskrit and Pali) into another language not at first his own (English). His aim – decried by some academic critics but appreciated by thousands of readers all over the world – was to convey the essence of the original in pure, poetic English . . . His translations ⎯⎯⎯⎯⎯⎯⎯⎯⎯ *apada* are the best that we ⎯⎯⎯⎯⎯⎯⎯⎯⎯ be superseded.'

THE UPANISHADS

TRANSLATIONS FROM THE SANSKRIT

WITH AN INTRODUCTION BY

JUAN MASCARÓ

PENGUIN BOOKS

PENGUIN BOOKS

Published by the Penguin Group
Penguin Books Ltd, 27 Wrights Lane, London W8 5TZ, England
Viking Penguin, a division of Penguin Books USA Inc.
375 Hudson Street, New York, New York 10014, USA
Penguin Books Australia Ltd, Ringwood, Victoria, Australia
Penguin Books Canada Ltd, 2801 John Street, Markham, Ontario, Canada L3R 1B
Penguin Books (NZ) Ltd, 182–190 Wairau Road, Auckland 10, New Zealand

Penguin Books Ltd, Registered Offices: Harmondsworth, Middlesex, England

First published 1965
20

Copyright © Juan Mascaró, 1965
All rights reserved

Printed in England by Clays Ltd, St Ives plc
Set in Linotype Pilgrim

CONTENTS

Thou art That (you are
what you r)

INTRODUCTION

THE Sanskrit word *Upanishad*, *Upa-ni-shad*, comes from the verb *sad*, to sit, with *upa*, connected with Latin *s-ub*, under; and *ni*, found in English be-*neath* and *ne*-ther. The whole would mean a sitting, an instruction, the sitting at the feet of a master. When we read in the Gospels that Jesus 'went up into a mountain : and when he was set, his disciples came unto him' we can imagine them sitting at the feet of their Master and the whole Sermon on the Mount might be considered an *Upanishad*.

The *Upanishads* are spiritual treatises of different length, the oldest of which were composed between 800 and 400 B.C. Their number increased with time and about 112 *Upanishads* have been printed in Sanskrit. Some were composed as late as the fifteenth century A.D. These repeat most of the ideas of the older *Upanishads*, using them for a particular school of thought or religious instruction. The longest and perhaps the oldest *Upanishads* are the *Brihad-aranyaka* and the *Chandogya* which cover about one hundred pages each, while the *Isa Upanishad*, one the most important, not far in age from the *Bhagavad Gita*, has only eighteen verses.

If all the known *Upanishads* were collected in one volume, they would make an Anthology about the length of the Bible. The spirit of the *Upanishads* can be compared with that of the New Testament summed up in the words 'I and my Father are one' and 'The kingdom of God is within you', the seed of which is found in the words of the Psalms 'I have said : Ye are gods; and all of you are the children of the most High'.

The *Bhagavad Gita* could be considered an *Upanishad*; and at the end of each chapter we find a note added in later times which begins with the words : 'Here in the Upanishad of the glorious *Bhagavad Gita*'.

7

In theory, an *Upanishad* could even be composed in the present day: a spiritual *Upanishad* that would draw its life from the One source of religions and humanism and apply it to the needs of the modern world.

When prince Dara Shukoh, the son of the emperor Shah Jahan who built the Taj Mahal, was in Kashmir in 1640, he heard about the *Upanishads* and he had fifty of them translated into Persian. This translation was finished in 1657, and it was much later put into Latin by Anquetil Duperron and published in Paris in 1802. This was read by Schopenhauer, who said of the *Upanishads*: their reading 'has been the consolation of my life, and will be of my death' – '*Sie ist der Trost meines Lebens gewesen und wird der meines Sterbens sein.*'

In the songs of the *Vedas* we find the wonder of man before nature: fire and water, the winds and the storms, the sun and the rising of the sun are sung with adoration. They sometimes remind us of the love of nature of St Francis when he sings:

Glory be to thee, my God, for the gift of thy creation, and especially for our brother, the sun, who gives us the day and by whom thou givest us light. He is beautiful and radiant and of great glory, and bears witness to thee, O most High.

Glory be to thee, my God, for our brother the wind and the air, serene or in clouds and in all weathers, by which thou dost sustain all creatures.

Glory be to thee, my God, for our sister water, which is very useful and humble, and precious and pure.

Glory be to thee, my God, for our brother fire, by whom thou dost illumine the night; and he is beautiful, and joyful, and strong and full of power.

The songs of the *Vedas* cannot begin with 'Glory be to thee, my God', as the song of St Francis does, nor reach the sublime end of the song: 'Glory be to thee, my God, for those who forgive for love of thee' – '*Laudato si', mi Signore, per quelli che perdonano per lo tuo amore.*' The ascension from the many to the One was not yet complete in the *Vedas*, nor do we find in them the Spirit of love revealed in the *Svetasvatara Upanishad*, in Buddha, and in the *Bhagavad Gita*.

When in the *Vedas*, however, the soul of the poet is one with the god he is praising, we often find a sense of oneness, as if there were one God above all the gods, as when we hear these words to Varuna, the god of mercy:

We praise thee with our thoughts, O God. We praise thee even as the sun praises thee in the morning: may we find joy in being thy servants.

Keep us under thy protection. Forgive our sins and give us thy love.

God made the rivers to flow. They feel no weariness, they cease not from flowing. They fly swiftly like birds in the air.

May the stream of my life flow into the river of righteousness. Loose the bonds of sin that bind me. Let not the thread of my song be cut while I sing; and let not my work end before its fulfilment.   *Rig Veda* II. 28

In one of the latest songs of the *Vedas*, the song to *Purusha*, we find that the god is described in words that remind us of the Brahman of the *Upanishads*:

Purusha is the whole universe: what has been and what is going to be. One fourth of him is all beings, three fourths of him is immortal heaven.

And when the poet of the *Vedas* sings the glory of Vata, the god of the winds, he says: 'Spirit of the gods, seed of all the worlds', '*Ātmā devānām, bhuvanasya garbho*'.

We also find in the *Vedas* some of those supreme questions, asked by man when he considers the meaning of this great All, which were to be answered later on in the *Upanishads*:

There was not then what is nor what is not. There was no sky, and no heaven beyond the sky. What power was there? Where? Who was that power? Was there an abyss of fathomless waters?

There was neither death nor immortality then. No signs were there of night or day. The ONE was breathing by its own power, in infinite peace. Only the ONE was: there was nothing beyond.

Darkness was hidden in darkness. The all was fluid and formless. Therein, in the void, by the fire of fervour arose the ONE.

And in the ONE arose love: Love the first seed of the soul. The truth of this the sages found in their hearts: seeking in their hearts with wisdom, the sages found that bond of union between Being and non-being.

Who knows the truth? Who can tell whence and how arose this universe? The gods are later than its beginning: who knows therefore whence comes this creation?

Only that god who sees in highest heaven: he only knows whence came this universe, and whether it was made or uncreated. He only knows, or perhaps he knows not.

Rig Veda x. 129

The ritual of adoration in the *Vedas*, when men felt the glory of this world and prayed for light, must in time have become the routine of prayers of darkness for the riches of this world. We find in the *Upanishads* a reaction against external religion; and when ideas of the *Vedas* are accepted they are given a spiritual interpretation. It is the permanent struggle between the letter that kills and the spirit that gives life. We thus read in the *Mundaka Upanishad*.

But unsafe are the boats of sacrifice to go to the farthest shore; unsafe are the eighteen books where the lower actions are explained.

In the *Bhagavad Gita* the same idea is even more powerfully expressed:

As is the use of a well of water where water everywhere overflows, such is the use of all the Vedas to the seer of the Supreme.

In different words the *Svetasvatara Upanishad* tells us:

Of what use is the *Rig Veda* to one who does not know the Spirit from whom the *Rig Veda* comes?

*

The composers of the *Upanishads* were thinkers and poets, they had the vision of the poet; and the poet knows well that if poetry takes us away from a lower reality of daily life it is only to lead us to the vision of a higher Reality even in this daily life, where limitations give way for the poet to the joy of liberation.

These compositions are as much above the mere archaeological curiosity of some scholars as light is above its definition. Scholarship is necessary to bring us the fruits of ancient wisdom, but only an elevation of thought and emotion can help us to enjoy them and transform them into life.

One of the messages of the *Upanishads* is that the Spirit can only be known through union with him, and not through mere learning. And can any amount of learning make us feel love, or see beauty or hear the 'unheard melodies'? Some have only seen the variety of thought in the *Upanishads*, not their underlying unity. To them the words in the sacred texts might be applied: 'Who sees variety and not the unity wanders on from death to death'.

The spirit of the *Upanishads* is the Spirit of the Universe. Brahman, God himself, is their underlying spirit. The Christian must feel that Brahman is God, and the Hindu must feel that God is Brahman. Unless a feeling of reverence independent of the barriers of names can be felt for the Ineffable, the saying of the *Upanishads* is true: 'Words are weariness', the same idea expressed by the prophet that 'Of making many books there is no end'.

'The Holy Spirit' may be the nearest translation of Brahman in Christian language. Whilst God the Father and God the Son are in the foreground of the mind of many Christians, the Holy Spirit seems to receive less adoration. And in India the Brahman of the *Upanishads* is not as popular as Siva, Vishnu, or Krishna. Even Brahma, the manifestation of Brahman as creator, and not to be confused with him, is not living in the daily devotions of the Hindu, as are the two other gods of the trinity, Siva and Vishnu. The *Upanishad* doctrine is not a religion of the many; but rather the

Spirit behind all religions is their central theme repeated in such a wonderful variety of ways.

Brahman in the Universe, God in his transcendence and immanence is also the Spirit of man, the Self in every one and in all, Atman. Thus the momentous statement is made in the *Upanishads* that God must not be sought as something far away, separate from us, but rather as the very inmost of us, as the higher Self in us above the limitations of our little self. In rising to the best in us we rise to the Self in us, to Brahman, to God himself. Thus when the sage of the *Upanishads* is pressed for a definition of God, he remains silent, meaning that God is silence. When asked again to express God in words, he says: '*Neti, neti*', 'Not this, not this'; but when pressed for a positive explanation he utters the sublimely simple words: 'TAT TVAM ASI', 'Thou art That'.

According to the *Upanishads*, the reality of God can only be apprehended in a consciousness of joy that is beyond ordinary consciousness. The silent voice of the Eternal is perpetually whispering in us his melodies everlasting. The radiance of the Infinite is everywhere, but our ears cannot hear and our eyes cannot see: the Eternal cannot be grasped by the transient senses or the transient mind. This is beautifully expressed in the *Taittiriya Upanishad*: 'Words and mind go to him, but reach him not and return. But he who knows the joy of Brahman fears no more.'

Only the Eternal in us can lead us to the Eternal, only when the transient has become Eternal can a man say: 'I am He'.

Brahman is described as immanent and transcendent, within all and outside all. If the All is imagined as a triangle, the apex might be imagined as God transcendent, who in his expansion creates matter out of himself, not out of nothing, and thus becomes immanent until the end of evolution when the immanent has all again become transcendent in an ascension of evolution towards him. Why? For the joy of creation. Why is there evil? For the joy of good arising from it. Why darkness? That light may shine the more. Why suffering? For the instruction of the soul and the joy of sacrifice. Why the infinite play of creation and evolution? For *Anandam*, pure joy.

In the rising from non-Self to Self, from unconsciousness to consciousness, and from this to supreme Consciousness, there is a process of unselfishness. The more the lower self is forgotten in good works, and in the realization of the beautiful and the true, the quicker becomes the process of evolution.

The self-training for the vision of the unity of Atman and Brahman is called Yoga. Later on it was developed with such a wealth of detail and observation that its study should offer much deep interest to the Western psychologist. In the *Upanishads* is found the conception of a fourth state of consciousness, above waking, dreaming and deep sleep.

The law of evolution called Karma explains the apparent injustice in the world with sublime simplicity. There is a law of cause and effect in the moral world. We are the builders of our own destiny, and the results are not limited to one life, since our Spirit that was never born and will never die must come again and take to itself a body, that the lower self may have the reward of its works. Good shall lead to good, and evil to evil. From good, joy shall come, and from evil shall come suffering. And thus the great evolution flows on towards perfection.

There are two points that seem to have puzzled readers of these sacred texts: the problem of personality, and of the final union with Brahman.

It has been thought that because matter and the lower personality have only a relative reality, later on to be called *maya* – illusion, something that passes away and is not eternal reality – our personality, that personality so dear to us, has been considered unimportant and neglected.

Does it mean, because Shakespeare transformed his mind into a thousand minds, because in his all-embracing sympathy he became for a time a Hamlet or a Falstaff, that his personality is forgotten? In the process of creation the little self is forgotten, only to emerge much greater in the march towards the Eternal; the transient is left behind, but the transient becomes Eternal. 'Who knows God becomes God', says the *Mundaka Upanishad*.

And when all the transient has been left behind, when final liberation has been attained, when our little self is lost in the greater Self in us and in all, as a drop of water is lost in the sea, does it mean that all consciousness is lost? After the death of the lower self, when the small drop of human consciousness has become one with the ocean of Consciousness, when in the suggestive words of the *Brihad-aranyaka Upanishad* the seer is alone in an ocean, '*Salila eko drastād-vaito bhavati*', does it mean that consciousness is lost? Yes, says Yajñavalkya to his wife in the same *Upanishad*; for 'How can the Knower be known?' But does not this mean that the little self has then become the Self supreme and not only has the consciousness of his long experience, but has access to the Consciousness of all, not only has the book of his own past, but also the Book of the Universe?

How could the union with God be unconsciousness, unless God was unconsciousness? In the image of St Teresa, the silkworm has died and has become a beautiful butterfly. Free from its limitations, the little self forgets its limited life in the boundless ocean of life. It is not a death, but a victory over death, a rising and a resurrection.

So little is this our life neglected in the *Upanishads* that on our actions during this life depends all our future life, and even life everlasting. So important is this life that in the *Katha Upanishad* it is stated that the Spirit can only be seen in this life, or in the highest heaven, but not in the regions of the departed or in the lower heavens. The importance given to this life is clear behind the symbolism.

The joy of the final union is felt by St John of the Cross when he describes the Beloved as the 'silent music' and 'the sound of solitude'. And this final union is described by St Teresa in words that remind us of the *Upanishads* two thousand years before. It is like 'water falling from heaven into a

14

river or fountain, when all becomes water, and it is not possible to divide or separate the water of the river from that which fell from heaven; or when a little stream enters the sea so that henceforth there shall be no means of separation.' And in a different way it is the joy felt by Wordsworth, or by the greatest poet of the Catalan literary renaissance, Maragall, when he exclaims:

> Tot semblava un món en flor
> i l'ànima n'era jo.

'All seemed a world in flower, and I was the soul of this world.'

*

As the visions of the *Upanishads* are based on a consciousness of our own being in relation to the Being of the universe, whatever may be the mental progress of man upon this earth he can never go beyond the visions of the *Upanishads*: he can never go beyond himself, his own consciousness, his own life. Could he think if he were not alive?

Each one of us is a centre of life, a unique event in the universe, and whatever our external relations to people and things may be, the absolute fact remains that we have to live our inner life alone even as we have to die our own death: no one can live our own inner life for us; and no one can go through our own death. In the infinite struggle of man to know this world and the universe around him, and also to know the mind that allows him to think, he comes before the simple fact that life is above thought: when he sees a fruit he can think about the fruit, but in the end he must eat it if he wants to know its taste: the pleasure and nourishment he may get from eating the fruit is not an act of thought.

If we consider that food is necessary for life, that food is something material and that we do not live in a world of incorporeal spirits, we may think that the basis of life is material, that 'It rests on a material basis', and that before man can enjoy life he must eat and be alive. This is true, but many in power forgot this truth and piously thought that instead of bread they could give the stones of religious dogmas and pious consolations. It is no wonder that thinkers arose in fury and prophetic indignation, and believing that the material violence of power can only be fought by violence and power they gave a material gospel of faith in life, against the gospel of an external religion based, according to them, on fanaticism and selfish self-deception. Can we wonder? The words of Shylock may come to our mind: 'If a Jew wrong a Christian, what is his humility? revenge: if a Christian wrong a Jew what should his sufferance be by Christian example? why, revenge.' Or, as Macbeth said: 'It will have blood; they say, blood will have blood.'

We thus have the old law of an eye for an eye, and a tooth for a tooth, and violence against violence. This law is so much consciously or unconsciously accepted that when a historian writes about past events of men or nations we often feel that he takes this law for granted; and he therefore does not write from a point of view which is free in that love which breaks the old law, in that love which is infinite liberty.

A material view of the universe seems therefore quite possible, so much so that we might call it the general view of modern man, ruled by a modern mechanism based on scientific materialism.

But is this all? Is a rationalistic interpretation of the universe quite reasonable? Is a scientific humanism quite human or quite scientific?

The answer of the *Upanishads* is quite definite: ATMAN, the mystery of our life, the light of our soul, the love which is the source of infinite joy, the vision of the good and the beautiful which is the source of everything beautiful or good that man can create upon this earth, is something which is above reason and therefore it can never be attained by reason alone. And we hear the words of the *Upanishads*:

Not through much learning is the Atman reached, not through the intellect and sacred teaching.   *Katha Up.*

He comes to the thought of those who know him beyond

thought, not to those who imagine he can be attained by thought: he is unknown to the learned and known to the simple.   *Kena Up.*

Or, in the words of Jesus, seeds of spiritual life: 'Except ye be converted and become as little children, ye shall not enter into the kingdom of heaven.'

What does all this mean? That besides a material view of the universe that in the end reduces all to matter, or electrons, or energy, and our brain to a machine, a wonderful machine indeed but a part of a material body; and which reduces consciousness to an energy merely emanating from the brain, and of course non-existent in the universe apart from it; and which reduces the universe to a universe of quantity and intellectual abstractions where in the end all things are dust and fall into dust and death, we have a universe of spiritual radiance from which this universe of matter is only a reflection, a world of Spirit so much more wonderful to the soul than the physical universe is to the mind, the universe of eternal beauty which has been felt by all the greatest seers and poets and spiritual men of all times, where all things are in life and go into life. This led Bradley to say:

That the glory of this world in the end is appearance leaves the world more glorious, if we feel it is a show of some fuller splendour; but the sensuous curtain is a deception and a cheat, if it hides some colourless movement of atoms, some spectral woof of impalpable abstractions.

And Rabindranath Tagore can write with faith:

For the world is not atoms or molecules or radio-activity or other forces, the diamond is not carbon, and light is not vibrations of ether. You can never come to the reality of creation by contemplating it from the point of view of destruction.

And Shelley, speaking of poetry, can say:

It is at once the centre and circumference of knowledge; it is that which comprehends all science, and that to which all science must be referred. It is as the odour and the colour of the rose to the texture of the elements which compose it, as the form and splendour of unfaded beauty to the secrets of anatomy and corruption.

The world of modern science is becoming more and more interesting, more poetical, and therefore more spiritual; but it is still concerned with matter. We are on the threshold of this great world of science and who knows the wonders the mind of man can discover? But however far the mind of man can go there will still be the tremendous assertion of the *Taittiriya Upanishad*: 'Words and mind go to Him, but reach Him not and return. But he who knows the joy of Brahman, fears no more.' Or, in the words of the *Kaushitaki Upanishad*: 'It is not thought which we should want to know: we should know the thinker.'

A flower can be an object of trade: something to buy and sell for money. This is its lowest value. It can also be an object of intellectual interest, but then it becomes an abstraction and from a purely intellectual point of view a nettle may sometimes be more interesting than a flower. But to the soul the flower is an object of joy, and to the poet it can be a thing of beauty and truth: a window from which we may look in wonder into the Beauty and Truth of the universe, and the Truth and Beauty in our own souls. Blake saw this when he wrote:

> To see a World in a grain of sand,
> And a Heaven in a wild flower,
> Hold Infinity in the palm of your hand,
> And Eternity in an hour.

All things on earth, from a flower to a human being, can be an object of love or contemplation, an object of intellectual interest, and an object of possession. In the first case they give us the freedom of joy in the Infinite; in the second they give us that knowledge which is power; in the third they give us the chains that bind us to matter, drag us down to the darkness of death, to the miseries of competition for selfish power, instead of cooperation for unselfish joy. Those three attitudes of mind, those three types of knowledge, are well described in the *Bhagavad Gita*:

When one sees Eternity in things that pass away and Infinity in finite things, then one has pure knowledge.

But if one merely sees the diversity of things, with their divisions and limitations, then one has impure knowledge.

And if one selfishly sees a thing as if it were everything, independent of the ONE and the many, then one is in the darkness of ignorance. XVIII. 20–22

What a wonderful relation do we establish with a human being when in spite of his limitations we see his Infinity! But if we merely consider him as an object of intellectual curiosity, a fixed number in static statistics, or even as a mere machine whose work we can buy and sell, we degrade both him and ourselves.

'Know thyself' is supreme wisdom; but how can we know ourselves? Is it a mere intellectual knowledge that we want? Modern psychology may explain a good many of the *workings* of the mind and make interesting and helpful guesses; but this is a study of the mind as an *object*. How can the mind be known as a subject, except by experience? We all know different values in our inner life: the difference of inner life when the routine of daily tribulations, great or small, makes us feel that we are not really living, or when we hear a symphony of Beethoven, or read Shakespeare or Dante or the *Upanishads*, if we can read or listen; but can we know what allows us to be conscious of our own consciousness? Can we know that essence of our life which allows us to live and to feel and to think? If we did, we would then know ourselves, our Atman, we would know God. We could then know, even as we know that we are alive but with a far greater intensity, that there is a centre in us which gives us that oneness which we call consciousness and that can be one with the ONE, the invisible link that gives the unity of our little lives and is the oneness of this vast universe.

This is the great adventure and the great discovery. No one can do it for us. Until we have reached the top of the mountain we cannot see in full glory the view that lies beyond; but glimpses of light illumine our path to the mountain. These glimpses of light give us faith, because then we know, not with the external knowledge of reading books, but with that certainty of faith that comes from moments of inner life. But if in intellectual pride or in the laziness of dullness we deny the light, thereby denying ourselves, how can we avoid being in darkness?

This is why the greatest prayers of men have always been prayers for light and love. We cannot buy light and love in the market place of men; but they are given to us 'without money and without price'.

In the external world where our body moves and has its life we are not free. We have to obey the laws of nature, the laws of God, or we suffer; and it is the task of our intellect gradually to discover those laws. But there is our little world of inner life. Here we have limited freedom, but we are free enough to deny the light and even to deny God. Here in our inner world there is something which is not bound by the laws of nature, by the laws of time and space. In the inmost of our soul there is the world of the Spirit and the world of the Spirit is free: 'Where the Spirit of the Lord is, there is liberty.' But the more we deny the Spirit of the Lord, our Atman, our own Self, the more are we bound. We could live in the centre of our soul and thus feel the infinite joy of Brahman, but instead of yearning towards the centre we make infinite centres of selfishness in the circumference of our souls. The farther those centres are from the Centre, the farther we are from the light: selfishness becomes stronger and stronger, the chains that bind us and which we so laboriously make with our thoughts and works are more and more difficult to break. In the struggle for goods that can give pleasure and power we clash with others who also want power and pleasure, and instead of a cooperation in love that would lead to the joy of light we have the vast competition that leads down to darkness and destruction. Why should men worry about the 'why?' of evil and ugliness when so much of the ugliness and evil of this world is the work of man? This is why Buddha refused to answer metaphysical questions: he gave the path of love that leads to Nirvana, the Kingdom of Heaven, where all questions shall be answered, and the answer will be life.

Our Masters of the spiritual life want us to be at least as practical in the work that leads to joy as others are 'practical' in the work that leads to the illusion of self-exaltation. 'Seek ye first the kingdom of God, and his righteousness; and all these things shall be added unto you', says Jesus whose words are Truth, and he also says, 'Behold the kingdom of God is within you'. We pray 'Thy kingdom come', and the kingdom of heaven is at hand; but we also pray 'Thy will be done', and what is the will but the will of love? The Truth of the Spirit is not found by the arguing of philosophical or metaphysical questions. How can we ask a question about something so near at hand? It is as if we were asking whether we are alive; and in fact we might well ask this question since so much of our life is mere vegetable or animal life. We know that we are alive, but not alive to the Highest Life. If, however, we are tempted to argue about the supreme problems, forgetting the words of Indian wisdom that 'Those things which are beyond thought should not be subjected to argument' and that 'When we can argue about a thing it shows that it is not worth arguing about', we may listen to the words of Buddha:

Imagine a man that has been pierced by an arrow well soaked in poison, and his relatives and friends go at once to fetch a physician or a surgeon. Imagine now that this man says:

'I will not have this arrow pulled out until I know the name of the man who shot it, and the name of his family, and whether he is tall or short or of medium height; until I know whether he is black or dark or yellow; until I know his village or town. I will not have the arrow pulled out until I know about the bow that shot it, whether it was a long bow or a cross bow.

I will not have this arrow pulled out until I know about the bow-string, and the arrow, and the feathers of the arrow, whether they are feathers of vulture, or kite or peacock.

I will not have the arrow pulled out until I know whether the tendon which binds it is of an ox, or deer, or monkey.

I will not have this arrow pulled out until I know whether it is an arrow, or the edge of a knife, or a splinter, or the tooth of a calf, or the head of a javelin.'

Well, that man would die, but he would die without having found out all these things.

In the same way, any one who would say: 'I will not follow the holy life of Buddha until he tells me whether the world is eternal or not; whether the life and the body are two things, or one thing; whether the one who has reached the Goal is beyond death or not; whether he is both beyond death and not beyond death; whether he is neither beyond death nor is not beyond death.'

Well, that man would die, but he would die without Buddha having told these things.

Because I am one who says: Whether the world is eternal or not, there is birth, and death, and suffering, and woe, and lamentation, and despair. And what I do teach is the means that lead to the destruction of these things.

Remember therefore that what I have said, I have said; and that what I have not said, I have not said. And why have I not given an answer to these questions? Because these questions are not profitable, they are not a principle of the holy life, they lead not to peace, to supreme wisdom, to Nirvana.

Majjhima Nikaya 1. 63

Yes, our spiritual life is a vision and a creation: doubts and unprofitable questions do not help. We have to build our inner house. Blake who saw, as perhaps no one else has better seen, the relation between spiritual vision and poetry, expressed this idea in these words:

I must create a system, or be enslaved by another man's;
I will not reason and compare: my business is to create.

Our spiritual life must be a work of creation. Whether we are within a religion, or outside a religion, or against religion, we can only live by faith, a burning faith in the spiritual values of man. This faith can only come from life, from the deep fountain of life within us, the Atman of the *Upanishads*, Nirvana, the Kingdom of Heaven. A deep faith in life cannot but be spiritual, even if only partially spiritual. That is why the faith in science and in man that makes men speak of 'One for all and all for one'; 'Man is to man a friend and a brother'; 'Honesty and truthfulness, moral purity and modesty' is a faith that cannot be material because it comes from the Spirit within us. A scientific humanism based on science, if illumined by love and the light of beauty, is bound to lead to the Atman of the *Upanishads*, to the glory of the Spirit in man. The path of Truth may not be a path of parallel lines but a path that follows one circle: by going to the right and climbing the circle, or by going to the left and climbing the circle we are bound to meet at the top, although we started in apparently contrary directions. This is bound to be in the end, because Truth is one. This is expressed in the *Bhagavad Gita*, the Song of God:

In any way that men love me in that same way they find my love: for many are the paths of men, but they all in the end come to me.

And when Keats was only twenty-two years old he could write deep thoughts that have a curious similarity to ideas in the *Mundaka Upanishad* and the verse of the *Gita* just quoted:

Now it appears to me that almost any Man may like the spider spin from his own inwards his own airy Citadel – the points of leaves and twigs on which the spider begins her work are few, and she fills the air with a beautiful circuiting. Man should be content with as few points to tip with the fine Web of his Soul, and weave a tapestry empyrean – full of symbols for his spiritual eye, of softness for his spiritual touch, of space for his wanderings, of distinctness for his luxury. But the minds of mortals are so different and bent on such diverse journeys that it may at first appear impossible for any common taste and fellowship to exist between two or three under these suppositions. It is however quite the contrary. Minds would leave each other in contrary directions, traverse each other in numberless points, and at last greet each other at the journey's end. An old man and a child would talk together and the old man be led on his path and the child left thinking. Man should not dispute or assert, but whisper results to his Neighbour, and thus by every germ of spirit sucking the sap from mould ethereal every human might become great, and humanity instead of being a wide heath of furze and briars, with here and there a remote Oak or Pine, would become a great democracy of forest trees.

All men of good will are bound to meet if they follow the wisdom of the words of Shakespeare in *Hamlet* where, if we write SELF for *self*, we find the doctrine of the *Upanishads*:

> This above all, – to thine own self be true;
> And it must follow, as the night the day,
> Thou canst not then be false to any man.

*

There are two ideas around which the deepest problems of thought and of all spiritual vision and life revolve: the idea of Being and the idea of Love.

The central vision of the *Upanishads* is Brahman, and although Brahman is beyond thoughts and words, he can be felt by each one of us as Atman, as our own being. The words of Hamlet, which are applied to a definite dramatic situation but which have, as so often in Shakespeare, a meaning far beyond their context, express the great problem:

TO BE, OR NOT TO BE: THAT IS THE QUESTION.

That is the question. Is there an infinite Being in the universe within and beyond the vastness of space and the revolutions of the stars? Is there an eternal Being behind the perpetual movement of our minds and the beatings of our heart of life? Because if there were not this Being we could never be: we could only be a perpetual becoming until our end in dust.

The answer of the *Upanishads* is YES, and this means that the essence of the universe and of ourselves is positive: it is the holy word of the *Upanishads*, OM, one of the meanings of which is YES. How can we know? This Truth can be known in the silence of the soul. We are told again and again that in the deep silence of the soul man can be in union with himself: not with his transitory consciousness, not with the apparent nothingness of deep sleep, not with the vagueness of dreams; but when man is in union with the background of his consciousness, the centre of his soul, then he is in union with himself, his own Self: only when man is in union with God is he in union with himself, one with himself and with all creation. Then he sees by that inner light which is in the secret place of his soul, in that place where, in the words found in the *Katha*, *Mundaka* and *Svetasvatara Upanishads*:

There the sun shines not, nor the moon, nor the stars; lightnings shine not there and much less earthly fire. From his light all these give light, and his radiance illumines all creation.

Then the words of Isaiah become true for that soul:

The sun shall be no more thy light by day, neither for brightness shall the moon give light unto thee: but the Lord shall be unto thee an everlasting light, and thy God thy glory.

Glimpses of this joy of Being are found in all great poets, and Wordsworth can say:

> Our noisy years seem moments in the being
> Of the eternal silence.

The joy that irradiates the poetry of the great modern Spanish poet Jorge Guillén springs from the joy of Being:

> Ser, nada más. Y basta.
> Es la absoluta dicha.

'To be. No more. This is all. This is the joy supreme.'

Wordsworth felt the Brahman of the *Upanishads*. That is why he can write in the first edition of *The Prelude*:

> I felt the sentiment of Being spread
> O'er all that moves, and all that seemeth still,
>
> ...Wonder not
> If such my transports were; for in all things now
> I saw one life and felt that it was joy.

This is the pure spirit of the *Upanishads*. Later on he descended to a less poetical religion and suppressing what is perhaps the most sublime verse in all his poetry – 'I saw one life, and felt that it was joy' – he wrote:

> Wonder not
> If high the transport, great the joy I felt,
> Communing in this sort through earth and heaven
> With every form of creature, as it looked
> Towards the Uncreated with a countenance
> Of adoration, with an eye of love.

The two versions reveal that the truly spiritual is always poetical: the Lord wants to be worshipped in the beauty of holiness. The words of the prayer which Jesus taught, 'Hallowed be thy name', express this truth.

The two versions also reveal that the truly spiritual comes from the power of a high Imagination, not from weak pious beliefs, nor from intellectual activities of the mind. Theology may help to make clear our thoughts, but its relation to spiritual vision is that of grammar to living language, or of poetics to soul-uplifting poetry. The spiritual vision, like the poetical vision, is not an analysis, it is not even a synthesis: it is the joy of truth revealed to a living soul.

Every spiritual and poetical vision comes from imagination: because imagination is the light of the soul. Without imagination we cannot have faith, because 'Faith is the substance of things hoped for, the evidence of things not seen': things not seen of course by reason or by the eyes of the body, but seen by the spirit. Without imagination there is no vision and no creation. Most of the miseries of man, such as selfishness, injustice, and cruelty, have their root in a lack of imagination. But imagination is not fancy. As Rabindranath Tagore says, 'The stronger is the imagination, the less imaginary it is'. Fancies disturb the mind and they may lead to destruction; but imagination is an inner light which with the help of reason leads to construction. All faith comes from true imagination, but fancy, or distorted imagination, is the source of all fanaticism and superstition. Since faith and fanaticism, imagination and fancy, vision and superstition are so much intermingled in the history of religions, it is no wonder that those who, through lack of spiritual discrimination, cannot see the difference between faith based on vision and fear based on superstition may be bound by a merely external religion or condemn all religion.

It was the splendour of a poetical imagination that inspired the greatest poetry of Blake and Wordsworth, of Coleridge and Shelley and Keats. Wordsworth could say that 'Spiritual love acts not nor can exist without imagination' and in *The Prelude* when he describes the crossing of the Alps he can give us a splendid vision where imagination and faith are one:

> Imagination – here the Power so-called
> Through sad incompetence of human speech,
> That awful Power rose from the mind's abyss
> Like an unfathered vapour that enwraps,
> At once, some lonely traveller. I was lost;
> Halted without an effort to break through;
> But to my conscious soul I now can say –
> 'I recognize thy glory'; in such strength
> Of usurpation, when the light of sense
> Goes out, but with a flash that has revealed
> The invisible world, doth greatness make abode,
> There harbours; whether we be young or old,
> Our destiny, our being's heart and home,
> Is with infinitude, and only there;
> With hope it is, hope that can never die,
> Effort, and expectation, and desire,
> And something evermore about to be.

Coleridge describes Imagination in words that could be applied to the Brahman of the *Upanishads*:

The primary Imagination I hold to be the living power and prime agent of all human perception, and as a repetition in the finite mind of the eternal act of creation in the infinite I AM.

And his description of 'secondary Imagination' might be applied to the Atman, our soul:

The secondary Imagination I consider an echo of the former, co-existing with the conscious will, yet still as identical with the primary in the *kind* of its agency, and differing only in *degree*, and in the *mode* of its operation.

Coleridge's description of fancy as 'a mode of memory' with 'fixities and definites' shows us how visions which are creations of faith can become in minds without imagination the 'fixities and definites' of fanaticism:

Fancy, on the contrary, has no other counters to play with, but fixities and definites. The fancy is indeed no other than a mode of memory emancipated from the order of time and space.

How can we know the true light of the higher Imagination from the distorted wanderings of fancies? This is the task of wisdom, of a wisdom that is not taught in schools. 'Watch and pray' can lead us on our path. When we watch in inner silence and our prayer is love, light shines, since the light of our Atman is ever in us. Just as in literary criticism we slowly learn to distinguish the true from the false, the good from the less good, our spiritual criticism can be developed so that we can distinguish true spiritual values from their imitations; and then we can choose the guides of our spiritual life. The *Upanishads* and all great spiritual masters warn us of the wrong teachers. 'He cannot be taught by one who has not reached Him', says the *Katha Upanishad*; and Jesus repeatedly warns us against false teachers and pharisees: 'If the blind lead the blind, both shall fall into the ditch.' All help from outside, whether from books or from men, must pass the test of our reason and of our own spiritual watch and prayer. A Master is ever in us, as Ramanuja says:

> Thou my mother, and my father Thou.
> Thou my friend, and my teacher Thou.
> Thou my wisdom, and my riches Thou.
> Thou art all to me, O God of all gods.

*

From the idea of Brahman found in its most pure form in the oldest *Upanishads*, we find in the *Isa Upanishad*, and especially in the *Svetasvatara Upanishad*, an evolution towards that idea of God afterwards to be developed in full splendour in the *Bhagavad Gita*. When Krishna, as God, speaks to Arjuna in the *Gita* he says,

> By love he knows me in truth, who I am and what I am. And when he knows me in truth he enters into my Being.   18. 55

He uses in Sanskrit the words 'viśate Tad Anantaram', 'enters into That Eternal – my Being' and this reminds us of the 'TAT TVAM ASI', 'That thou art' of the *Upanishads*. The suggestion is that Brahman is the Being of God, even as God is the centre of our Being. God beyond creation is Brahman. Brahman in the universe is God. In the first case Brahman is beyond the historical ever-changing process of the universe, even as our Atman is beyond our 'childhood, youth and old age', as the *Gita* sings. In the second case Brahman is the God of the universe, ever watching and helping the work of creation, the God who is in the centre of our hearts, whom we can love and, what is even more wonderful, whose love we can feel.

And what is love? We know that it cannot be defined. The words of Lao Tzu remind us of this truth, if instead of his word TAO we use the word GOD or LOVE.

People think that Tao is foolishness because it lacks definition: But Tao lacks definition because it is infinite. If Tao could be defined, it would be small and not great.

And if we want to argue about the nature of love, the words of Lao Tzu also come to our mind:

> He who loves does not dispute:
> He who disputes does not love.

That is why we find love expressed by contradictions, by those efforts of the human mind when words cannot be found for the Ineffable. Ramon Llull, the great medieval spiritual thinker and poet of the Island of Majorca, 1235–1316, who knew what love is, could say:

Love is that which places the free in bondage and to those in bondage gives freedom.

We think we are free, but in our darkness

> The heart-ache, and the thousand natural shocks
> That flesh is heir to

keep us in perpetual bondage; and all the longing and yearning expressed by the German word *Sehnsucht* or the Catalan word *anyorança* are an expression of this bondage. Our soul longs for freedom, for the *mukti* of the *Upanishads*, for liberation. And where can the finite find freedom except in the Infinite? Where can the bird in a cage find freedom except in the infinite sky?

The light of Truth is the End of the journey. The path of the Upanishads is essentially the path of Light, the consciousness of Brahman which is far beyond all mental consciousness. This has been considered in the *Upanishads* the highest path and even in the *Bhagavad Gita* which is a gospel of love, and of works in love, the JÑĀNĪ, the man of vision, is placed above all men, because as Krishna says, 'The man of vision and I are one', '*Jñānī tv Ātma eva me matam*.' When by love the full communion of man with God has taken place, when man sees God in all and all in God, then that man is one with Brahman, he has crossed the river of life and he has heard the songs of immortality welcoming him on the other shore. This is what all the masters of the Spirit tell us.

When the End of wisdom is described in the *Bhagavad Gita* some of the words of the *Isa Upanishad* are used:

Now I shall tell thee of the End of Wisdom. When a man knows this he goes beyond death. It is Brahman, beginningless, supreme: beyond what is and beyond what is not.

He is invisible: he cannot be seen. He is far and he is near, he moves and he moves not, he is within all and he is outside all.

He is the Light of all lights which shines beyond all darkness. It is vision, the end of vision, to be reached by vision, dwelling in the hearts of all.   XIII. 12, 15, 17

And in the full spirit of the *Upanishads* the *Gita* says in words sublime:

He who sees that the Lord of all is ever the same in all that is, immortal in the field of mortality – he sees the truth.

And when a man sees that the God in himself is the same God in all that is, he hurts not himself by hurting others: then he goes indeed to the highest Path.   XIII. 27-28

In this way, as Paul Deussen says, the doctrine of the *Upanishads* explains and complements the doctrine of the Gospels, 'Thou shalt love thy neighbour as thyself'. Why? Because our Atman, our higher Self, dwells in us and dwells in our neighbour: if we love our neighbour, we love the God who is in us all and in whom we all are; and if we hurt our neighbour, in thought or in words or in deeds, we hurt ourselves, we hurt our soul: this is the law of spiritual gravitation.

Love is undefinable, but we know that love is joy: not indeed a transient pleasure, but an eternal joy of the soul. The *Katha Upanishad* speaks of the two paths:

There is the path of joy and there is the path of pleasure. Both attract the soul. The two paths lie in front of man. Pondering on them, the wise chooses the path of joy: the fool takes the path of pleasure.

It is the law of Karma, suggested in Omar Khayyám, where amongst the loveliness of roses and wine and earthly love we can find glimpses of the unearthly beauty found in the Sufis.

The Moving Finger writes; and, having writ,
Moves on: nor all your Piety nor Wit
Shall lure it back to cancel half a Line,
Nor all your Tears wash out a Word of it.

One of the tasks of education is to reveal the joy of the Infinite which is the joy of love. It is well expressed in the *Chandogya Upanishad*:

Where there is creation there is progress. Where there is no creation there is no progress: know the nature of creation.

Where there is joy there is creation. Where there is no joy there is no creation: know the nature of joy.

Where there is the Infinite there is joy. There is no joy in the finite.

All true progress is an inner creation that leads to the joy of the Infinite. When in the progress of our soul our God of love has been found then the words of beauty of the Sufis come true:

In this world I feel joyful because He is the source of joy: I am in love with all creation because He is the Creator.

I shall drink with joy the cup of sorrow because my Beloved is the cup-bearer: I will bear pain with gladness, because through Him I shall be healed.   SADI 1193-1291

Bergson compares the love of God for his creation to the love of creation that moves the soul of the artist. It is worth considering that whilst science makes concrete things abstract, art makes abstract things concrete: in the art of loving God the *Upanishads* lead us to a concrete God, so concrete that He is ever the very centre of our soul, the permanent background of our consciousness, the Life that gives life to our life. The passage of Bergson is interesting, because it is in the mystic, the poet of the Infinite, that we get a concrete God:

If the thinker wanted to use the words of the mystic, he could soon define the nature of God. God is love and also the end of love: herein we find the whole contribution of mysticism. The mystic will never grow tired of speaking of this twofold love.

His descriptions have no end, because what he wants to describe is undescribable. But he is definite on one point: that divine love is not something belonging to God: it is God Himself.

The thinker who holds God to be a person, and yet wishes to avoid anything like a gross assimilation with man, will do well to fasten on this point. He will think, for example, of the enthusiasm that can set a soul on fire, that can burn whatever is within, and henceforth only fill it wholly with itself. The person and the emotion are then one; and yet the person had never been his own self so much; and he is more simple, more unified, more himself.

Is there anything of more perfect structure, more elaborate, than a symphony of Beethoven? And yet all through the labour of arranging, rearranging, and selecting that took place on the intellectual plane the composer was striving towards a point beyond his intellectual plane where he could feel a sense of acceptance or rejection, a sense of direction, an inspiration. An indivisible emotion was living in that plane. No doubt the intellect was trying to express it in music, but the emotion itself was more than mere intellect and more than music. In contrast to a lower emotion which is below the intellect, that higher emotion was under the control of the will. An emotion of this kind doubtless resembles, however remotely, the sublime love which is for the mystic the very essence of God.

All mystics are unanimous in declaring that God has need of us, even as we have need of God. Why should God need us, unless it were to give us His love?

This is the conclusion to which the philosopher who accepts the mystical experience must come. The whole creation will then appear to him as a vast work of God for the creation of creators, for the possession of beings co-workers with Him and worthy of His love.   HENRI BERGSON 1859–1941

A song of love is heard as a background to all great prayers. Chaitanya, the great Indian mystic, A.D. 1500, pours out his heart in these words:

I pray not for wealth, I pray not for honours, I pray not for pleasures, or even the joys of poetry. I only pray that during all my life I may have love: that I may have pure love to love Thee.

And Kabir, 1440–1518, the Indian saint and poet, tells us: 'Listen to me, friend: he understands who loves.' For love is a beauty which is joy: a beauty which is truth. The truth of love is the Truth of the universe: it is the lamp of the soul that reveals the secrets of darkness.

And this love must be found in this life: that is the real message of the spiritual teachers. 'The kingdom of heaven is at hand', says Jesus. And in Ecclesiastes we find these words of wisdom:

Whatever thy hand findeth to do, do it with thy might; for there is no work, nor device, nor knowledge, nor wisdom, in the grave, whither thou goest.   9. 10

In the *Maitri Upanishad* we find a striking passage that shows that the idea of rebirth or reincarnation had already found a spiritual interpretation:

Samsara, the transmigration of life, takes place in one's mind. Let one therefore keep the mind pure, for what a man thinks that he becomes.

From a spiritual point of view what matters is not transmigration, or an after-death: what matters is immortality, and this is not a long life, or many lives, or a life after death. Immortality is Atman, the Spirit of Eternity within our mortal body and our mortal consciousness. Only in God there is immortality, 'beyond the birth and rebirth of life'. That is why the spiritual masters always give us a sense of practical wisdom. They do not want words: they want life, immortal life. When an Indian sage was asked, 'What is death?' he answered, 'I should ask: what is life?' Kabir expresses these thoughts in his simple and sublime way:

O friend! hope for Him whilst you live, know whilst you live, understand whilst you live: for in life deliverance abides.

If your bonds be not broken whilst living, what hope of deliverance in death?

It is but an empty dream, that the soul shall have union with Him because it has passed from the body:

34

If He is found now, He is found then. If not, we do but go to dwell in death.

Yes, this love which is the joy of the Infinite, the *ananda* of Brahman, this love that is God, is here and now. In the *Taittiriya Upanishad* Bhrigu Varuni asks his father to explain to him the mystery of Brahman, the mystery of the universe. His father speaks to him of the earth and the food of the earth, of life and the breath of life, of the mind and of reason, and of consciousness behind reason and mind. In the end Bhrigu Varuni saw the Truth expressed in these words sublime:

AND THEN HE SAW THAT BRAHMAN WAS JOY: FOR FROM JOY ALL BEINGS HAVE COME, BY JOY THEY ALL LIVE, AND UNTO JOY THEY ALL RETURN.

God is love, and love is joy. All the universe has come from love and unto love all things return.

*

Those who found light and love give us their help for our journey. They speak to us of a path. According to the *Katha Upanishad*, the path is 'narrow as the edge of a razor' or, in the words of Jesus, 'Narrow is the way which leadeth unto life'. And yet they all tell us that this narrow path leads to infinite freedom. Every step of light and love is a step towards a new life, a new view from the path that leads up to the mountain. The narrow path leads us safely through the jungle of life; but a moment comes when St John of the Cross can say: '*Ya por aquí no hay camino. Que para el justo no hay ley*', – 'And now there is no path here; since for the pure man there is no law.'

We find in the *Upanishads* more inspiration than definite teaching; but we find the beginnings of Yoga, of that communion of love and light which was going to be the main subject of the *Bhagavad Gita* and of a vast spiritual literature in India. Thus the *Katha Upanishad* tells us:

When the five senses and the mind are still, and reason itself rests in silence, then begins the Path supreme.

This calm steadiness of the senses is called Yoga. Then one should become watchful, because Yoga comes and goes.

In those two verses there is a suggestion of the prayer of recollection as described by St Teresa, leading to the prayer of quietness and the final prayer of union.

In the *Svetasvatara Upanishad* we find verses that sound very similar to those found in Chapter VI of the *Bhagavad Gita*:

With upright body, head and neck lead the mind and its powers into the heart; and the OM of Brahman will then be thy boat with which to cross the rivers of fear.

The OM of Brahman is here the love of God. In the *Gita*, devotion to Krishna, to God, is the chief means of concentration; and the silence of the soul is described in an image of beauty:

Then his soul is a lamp whose light is steady, for it burns in a shelter where no winds come.   6. 19

Just as the living words of Shakespeare are far above all the books that critics or scholars have written or may ever write on Shakespeare – critics have to write books on poets but poets do not write poems on critics – the living words of sacred books are infinitely above those of their commentators: the words of the *Upanishads* are far above those of the writers on Yoga. Analysis is of course necessary, since by analysis we 'observe, collect and classify', in fact we become clearly conscious of what may be a vague general impression; but we can only analyse by making abstractions, and we must ever return to life. Many intellectual books could be written on love by a man of keen intellect; but they would be merely intellectual books, and the writer might never have felt a flash of universal love. Most works on Yoga, beginning with the *Yoga Sutras* of Patanjali, those short definitions and spiritual rules worked out by a supremely great analytical mind, have their use; but we cannot see a country by merely looking at maps of the country, we cannot go on a journey if we merely stop at reading guides about the journey.

When the power of the intellect was applied to the spiritual ideas of the *Upanishads* and the *Gita*, it was found that there is a great relation between the mind and the body: that certain postures of the physical body helped concentration, and others hindered it, that our breath varies with our emotions, and that a deep quiet silent breath is a reflection of a quiet mind; and then the elaborate rules found in the teachings of Yoga were composed. All these teachings can be useful, but they can mislead the most sincere seeker of a spiritual path; because the path is the path of love, of love that leads to light. Once a single flash of love or light has illumined our darkness, there is one and only one thing to do, and this is summed up by St John of the Cross in the words 'Silence and work'. In one of his spiritual letters we read:

What is wanting, if indeed anything be wanting, is not writing or speaking – whereof ordinarily there is more than enough – but silence and work. For whereas speaking distracts, silence and action collect the thoughts, and strengthen the spirit. As soon therefore as a person understands what has been said to him for his good, he has no further need to hear or to discuss; but to set himself in earnest to practise what he has learnt with silence and attention.

Later in the letter he writes these words of light: 'Never fail, whatever may befall you, be it good or evil, to keep your heart quiet and calm in the tenderness of love.'

With this one sentence St John of the Cross explains the doctrine of the *Bhagavad Gita*. When in the *Gita* we read again and again that a man must be the same in heat or in cold, in pleasure or in pain, in victory or defeat, the meaning is, of course, that whatever may be the events of our outer or inner life we must ever have the peace of love: in fact that our life should perpetually breathe the air of love, since love is the living breath of the soul. And far from an evenness of love making us insensitive, it is that love which leads to that sublime state described in the *Bhagavad Gita*:

> And he is the greatest Yogi he whose vision is ever one: when the pleasure and pain of others is his own pleasure and pain.

Although love is the very first condition for entering the path, how can the waters of love be given to one who is not thirsty? That is why we find that meditation, longing and sorrow are the first prayers of the soul:

> As the hart panteth after the water brooks,
> So panteth my soul after thee, O God.

> My soul is athirst for God, for the living God:
> When shall I come and appear before God?

In the spirit of this longing we find the lovely prayer of Rabindranath Tagore:

> Day after day, O lord of my life, shall I stand before thee face to face? With folded hands, O lord of all worlds, shall I stand before thee face to face?

> Under thy great sky in solitude and silence, with humble heart shall I stand before thee face to face?

> In this laborious world of thine, tumultuous with toil and with struggle, among hurrying crowds, shall I stand before thee face to face?

> And when my work shall be done in this world, O king of kings, alone and speechless shall I stand before thee face to face?

There may be moments of desolation on the path of love but if even Jesus could say 'My soul is exceeding sorrowful, even unto death', need we be afraid? The words of the Hebrew prophet Habakkuk give expression to this faith:

> Although the fig tree shall not blossom, neither shall fruit be in the vines; the labour of the olive shall fail, and the fields shall yield no meat; the flock shall be cut off from the fold, and there shall be no herd in the stalls:
> Yet I will rejoice in the Lord, I will joy in the God of my salvation.

It is in the inner battle for concentrating on the higher, and thus rejecting the lower, that Yoga, psychology, philosophy, and wisdom can help. In his unequalled power of language Shakespeare can give us in Hamlet a vision of the man who is master of his fate:

> Since my dear soul was mistress of her choice,
> And could of men distinguish, her election
> Hath seal'd thee for herself: for thou hast been
> As one, in suffering all, that suffers nothing;
> A man that fortune's buffets and rewards
> Hast ta'en with equal thanks: and blest are those
> Whose blood and judgement are so well commingled,
> That they are not a pipe for fortune's finger
> To sound what stop she please. Give me that man
> That is not passion's slave, and I will wear him
> In my heart's core, ay, in my heart of heart,
> As I do thee.

When this power of self-control, and intelligence and mental energy are at the service of a good will, at the service of love, then a man can make quick progress on the path that leads to Brahman. When mental powers, and energy and self-control are not at the service of a good will, then history, literature, wisdom, and the daily events of the present world, tell us what are the results.

Any interest in Yoga, in miracles or psychic powers, not based on that humbleness of the soul which is the beginning and the end of all true spiritual light and love is at its best something of scientific interest, and at its worst it is that pride and desire for power which are the surest signs of spiritual darkness.

Let us take an interesting psychological experiment: thought-transmission or thought-reading. A person who knows something about hypnosis can easily ask a group of people to practise an exercise of relaxation whilst standing and then induce them to imagine that they are falling backwards or forwards. This quickly gives him an idea of those who are sensitive to auto-suggestion – all suggestion is auto-suggestion – and then the suggestions leading to a deep hypnotic sleep can be given. In the state of deep sleep a word or a number can be written on a paper and the person in deep sleep can be asked to read the word or the number placed behind him. The person in deep sleep reads accurately what is written, and when the same experiment is repeated with success several times with different words and numbers not the slightest doubt is left in the mind of the operator that thought-transmission, or thought-reading, is a fact. And when he hears long arguments to the contrary by those who of course have not practised the experiment he cannot but smile.

Well, what does the experiment prove? Only that, to quote Hamlet again,

> There are more things in heaven and earth, Horatio,
> Than are dreamt of in your philosophy.

But supposing that after this experiment we could attain all the psychic powers promised in Yoga, does this mean that we have advanced a single step on the spiritual path? Of course not. We have learnt something of amazing psychological interest; but we have not advanced on the path of love. We may even have gone backwards if the slightest pride or self-satisfaction has infected our mind.

Those who rely on physical miracles to prove the truth of spiritual things forget the ever-present miracle of the universe and of our own lives. The lover of the physical miracle is in fact a materialist: instead of making material things spiritual, as the poet or the spiritual man does, he simply makes spiritual things material, and this is the source of all idolatry and superstition. Leaving aside the question that matter and spirit may simply be 'different modes, or degrees in perfection, of a common *substractum*', as Coleridge says, and the *Upanishads* suggest, there is the far greater question that in everything spiritual there is an element of beauty which is truth, and which we find in faith, but which is lacking in fanaticism and superstition. The noble longing for truth of the scientist is exactly the same as the longing of the spiritual man for God, because God is Truth. The difference is that the scientist is busy finding facts in the outer world, whether in the stars that are millions of light-years from our little earth, or in the world discovered by the microscope; whilst the spiritual man is trying by the experience of Being and of Love to find the Truth of his inner world, the same Truth in the inner world of us all.

The external events of the world and the inner events of our minds are spiritually all *external* to our Atman, to our higher Self. They are things that happen in time and space. The nearer we are to that centre in us which is beyond time and space, the better can we watch those events and say 'They happen', as the *Gita* tells us, or as Jesus sums up in the eternal words 'Watch and pray'.

According to the mystics, it is important to know in prayer the difference between meditation and contemplation: meditation is a movement of thought limited within a circle, but in contemplation there is a silence of thought. Meditation is the mental activity of the thinker; contemplation is the silence of the poet. St Peter of Alcántara, 1499–1562, the Spanish saint who helped St Teresa, gives us in clear words the difference between the two:

In meditation we consider carefully divine things, and we pass from one to another, so that the heart may feel love. It is as though we should strike a flint, to draw a spark of fire.

But in contemplation the spark is struck: the love we were seeking is here. The soul enjoys silence and peace, not by many reasonings, but by simply contemplating the Truth.

Meditation is the means, contemplation is the end: the one is the path, the other is the end of the path. Even as the vessel is still and at rest when it has arrived in port, when the soul has reached contemplation through meditation it should cease its toils and inquiries; and happy in the vision of God, even as if He were present, be one in feelings of love, of wonder, of joy, or other such.

Let a man return into his own self, and there in the centre of his soul, let him wait upon God, as one who listens to another speaking from a high tower, as though he had God in his heart, as though in the whole creation there was only God and his soul.

If has been said that 'Prayer is perfect, when he who prays, remembers not that he is praying'.

Those beginners who try inner silence should, however, be careful to listen to the words of the true spiritual teachers. St Teresa, in her delightful human way, says that some people close their eyes and keep quiet and they think that this is 'ecstasy'. 'I do not call this *ecstasy, arrobamiento*', she says, 'I call it *stupidity, abobamiento*'. And she makes clear that the most sure sign of love is to do works of love. In her wonderful book 'Interior Castle' she writes:

When I see people very anxious to know what sort of prayer they practise, covering their faces and afraid to move or think, lest they should lose any slight tenderness and devotion they feel, I know now how little they understand how to obtain union with God, since they think it consists in such things as these.

No, sisters, no; our Lord expects *works* of us.

I have often spoken on this subject elsewhere, because, my sisters, if we fail in this I know all is lost; please God this may never be our case. If you possess fraternal charity, I assure you that you will certainly obtain the union I have described. If you are conscious that you are wanting in this charity, although you may feel devotion and sweetness and a short absorption in the prayer of quiet – which makes you think you have obtained the union with God – believe me you have not yet reached it. Beg our Lord to grant you perfect love for your neighbour, and leave the rest to Him. He will give you more than you know how to desire.

Amongst the signs that a nun who had 'visions' was simply in a state of *abobamiento*, St John of the Cross gives these: 1. Too much desire to enjoy visions. 2. Too much self-assurance. 3. A desire to convince others that she has a great good. 4. That those 'visions' have not given her a great sense of humbleness; and 5. That the style of her language shows that it is not the language of truth. And St

John of the Cross ends by saying: 'And all that she says that she said to God and God said to her seems absolute nonsense.'

A seeker of the Truth of life will seek the Truth of Being and of Love, since a single flash of this Truth gives us faith far stronger than life. This faith is confirmed by the words of sacred books, by the life of those whose life was a book of life, and by the inner whisperings of our soul.

Amongst the sacred books of the past, the *Upanishads* can be called in truth Himalayas of the Soul. Their passionate wanderings of discovery to find that sun of the Spirit in us, from whom we have the light of our consciousness and the fire of our life; the greatness of their questions, and the sublime simplicity of their answers; their radiance of joy when the revelation of the Supreme comes to their soul, and one of their poets can say, 'The light of the sun is my light'; their paradoxes and contradictions where we find a living truth; their simple stories where with concrete examples the greatest metaphysical truths are explained in the language of a child; their flashes of vision that reveal to us the infinite greatness of our inner world; their great variety and yet their absolute unity in the awe-inspiring conception of Brahman; their burning uplifting faith in the soul of man which is one with the Soul of the universe; their tolerance of the *Vedas*, but their spiritual and therefore symbolical interpretation of external ritual, thus showing the true path of spiritual upliftment to all men in times to come; their seeds of great psychological and philosophical ideas; the vast harmonies that ring through their words; their spiritual wisdom that can satisfy different minds in their search for light; their simple images which we find again in saints and poets of other ages who had never known of the *Upanishads*, and thus confirm to us the unity of all spiritual vision and life; the splendour of their romantic imagination that makes their creators brothers in spirit with the creators of beauty of all times, and which show us how to make our life a work of beauty: are all like trumpets

43

sounding the glory of light and love and, over the darkness of doubts and death, proclaiming the victory of life.

The Retreat,   JUAN MASCARÓ
Comberton, Cambridge
Summer 1964

NOTE ON THE TRANSLATIONS

THERE is much in the *Upanishads* which belongs to their own time. This has a historical interest, but not the spiritual value that belongs to all times. The same could be said of the Old Testament of the Bible.

That is why the spirit of the *Upanishads* can better be felt in a selection. I have translated the greatest *Upanishads* that happen not to be too long, and I have given the greatest passages of other *Upanishads*, including the sublime parts of the *Chandogya* and *Brihad-aranyaka Upanishads*. These are at the end of the book because, although in time they are the earliest, they lead the work to a culmination of greatness. The chronological order of the chief *Upanishads* is probably as follows: *Brihad-aranyaka, Chandogya, Taittiriya, Kaushitaki, Kena, Katha, Isa, Mundaka, Prasna, Mandukya, Svetasvatara,* and *Maitri.* I followed an Indian tradition by placing the *Isa Upanishad* at the beginning.

I took infinite pains to make the translations clear and simple. When an expression 'How can the Knower be known?' is a literal translation of the Sanskrit '*Vijñātāram are kena vijāīyāt?*' how a translator could say, 'Lo, whereby would one understand the understander?' is beyond my understanding!

This leads me to an earnest request to the reader of these translations: that they should be read aloud, whether orally or mentally. Unless they are, the meaning intended by the sound will be missed. This of course should always be done when one reads literature: if we say, for instance, $2 + 2 = 4$, our intellect grasps the inner meaning, and this is all that is necessary; but the words of Housman cannot be written in numbers:

> To think that two and two are four
> And neither five nor three

> The heart of man has long been sore
> And long 'tis like to be.

The *sound* of the numbers is in this case essential, since the sound is part of the meaning.

A good many of these translations were done over twenty-five years ago when I was living above Tintern Abbey, not far from the place that inspired Wordsworth's immortal poem. To the eighteen verses of the *Isa Upanishad* I devoted a whole month of thought and work.

The whole of the *Svetasvatara Upanishad* and other selections have been done during the last two years.

A few pages of the Introduction belong to the earlier work. As I could not improve them, I left them as they were. They are the second part of the five parts of the Introduction.

I hope that I have been true to the Spirit of the *Upanishads*, and thus to our own Spirit.

J.M.

ACKNOWLEDGEMENTS

I WISH to tender grateful acknowledgements to Messrs John Murray for so generously allowing me to use the translations from the *Upanishads* I made for them in the 'Wisdom of the East' series, and which were published in 1938 under the title *Himalayas of the Soul*. My gratitude is very sincere, as I do not think that I could have done the work again.

J.M.

THE UPANISHADS

ISA UPANISHAD

BEHOLD the universe in the glory of God: and all that lives and moves on earth. Leaving the transient, find joy in the Eternal: set not your heart on another's possession.

Working thus, a man may wish for a life of a hundred years. Only actions done in God bind not the soul of man.

There are demon-haunted worlds, regions of utter darkness. Whoever in life denies the Spirit falls into that darkness of death.

The Spirit, without moving, is swifter than the mind; the senses cannot reach him: He is ever beyond them. Standing still, he overtakes those who run. To the ocean of his being, the spirit of life leads the streams of action.

He moves, and he moves not. He is far, and he is near. He is within all, and he is outside all.

Who sees all beings in his own Self, and his own Self in all beings, loses all fear.

When a sage sees this great Unity and his Self has become all beings, what delusion and what sorrow can ever be near him?

The Spirit filled all with his radiance. He is incorporeal and invulnerable, pure and untouched by evil. He is the supreme seer and thinker, immanent and transcendent. He placed all things in the path of Eternity.

Into deep darkness fall those who follow action. Into deeper darkness fall those who follow knowledge.

One is the outcome of knowledge, and another is the outcome of action. Thus have we heard from the ancient sages who explained this truth to us.

He who knows both knowledge and action, with action overcomes death and with knowledge reaches immortality.

Into deep darkness fall those who follow the immanent. Into deeper darkness fall those who follow the transcendent.

One is the outcome of the transcendent, and another is the outcome of the immanent. Thus have we heard from the ancient sages who explained this truth to us.

He who knows both the transcendent and the immanent, with the immanent overcomes death and with the transcendent reaches immortality.

The face of truth remains hidden behind a circle of gold. Unveil it, O god of light, that I who love the true may see!

O life-giving sun, off-spring of the Lord of creation, solitary seer of heaven! Spread thy light and withdraw thy blinding splendour that I may behold thy radiant form: that Spirit far away within thee is my own inmost Spirit.

May life go to immortal life, and the body go to ashes. OM. O my soul, remember past strivings, remember! O my soul, remember past strivings, remember!

By the path of good lead us to final bliss, O fire divine thou god who knowest all ways. Deliver us from wandering evil. Prayers and adoration we offer unto thee.

KENA UPANISHAD

PART 1

WHO sends the mind to wander afar? Who first drives life to start on its journey? Who impels us to utter these words? Who is the Spirit behind the eye and the ear?

It is the ear of the ear, the eye of the eye, and the Word of words, the mind of mind, and the life of life. Those who follow wisdom pass beyond and, on leaving this world, become immortal.

There the eye goes not, nor words, nor mind. We know not, we cannot understand, how he can be explained: He is above the known and he is above the unknown. Thus have we heard from the ancient sages who explained this truth to us.

What cannot be spoken with words, but that whereby words are spoken: Know that alone to be Brahman, the Spirit; and not what people here adore.

What cannot be thought with the mind, but that whereby the mind can think: Know that alone to be Brahman, the Spirit; and not what people here adore.

What cannot be seen with the eye, but that whereby the eye can see: Know that alone to be Brahman, the Spirit; and not what people here adore.

What cannot be heard with the ear, but that whereby the ear can hear: Know that alone to be Brahman, the Spirit; and not what people here adore.

What cannot be indrawn with breath, but that whereby breath is indrawn: Know that alone to be Brahman, the Spirit; and not what people here adore.

PART 2

Master. If you think 'I know well', little truth you know.

You only perceive that appearance of Brahman that lies in the senses and is in you. Pursue your meditation.

Disciple. I mean to know.

I do not imagine 'I know him well', and yet I cannot say 'I know him not'. Who of us knows this, knows him; and not who says 'I know him not'.

He comes to the thought of those who know him beyond thought, not to those who imagine he can be attained by thought. He is unknown to the learned and known to the simple.

He is known in the ecstasy of an awakening which opens the door of life eternal. By the Self we obtain power, and by vision we obtain Eternity.

For a man who has known him, the light of truth shines; for one who has not known, there is darkness. The wise who have seen him in every being, on leaving this life, attain life immortal.

PART 3

Once upon a time, Brahman, the Spirit Supreme, won a victory for the gods. And the gods thought in their pride: 'We alone attained this victory, ours alone is the glory.'

Brahman saw it and appeared to them, but they knew him not. 'Who is that being that fills us with wonder?' they cried.

And they spoke to Agni, the god of fire: 'O god all-knowing, go and see who is that being that fills us with wonder.'

Agni ran towards him and Brahman asked: 'Who are you?' 'I am the god of fire,' he said, 'the god who knows all things.'

'What power is in you?' asked Brahman. 'I can burn all things on earth.'

And Brahman placed a straw before him, saying: 'Burn this.' The god of fire strove with all his power, but was unable to burn it. He then returned to the other gods and said: 'I could not find out who was that being that fills us with wonder.'

Then they spoke to Vayu, the god of the air. 'O Vayu, go and see who is that being that fills us with wonder.'

Vayu ran towards him and Brahman asked: 'Who are you?' 'I am Vayu, the god of the air,' he said, 'Matarisvan, the air that moves in space.'

'What power is in you?' asked Brahman. 'In a whirlwind I can carry away all there is on earth.'

And Brahman placed a straw before him saying: 'Blow this away.' The god of the air strove with all his power, but was unable to move it. He returned to the other gods and said: 'I could not find out who was that being that fills us with wonder.'

Then the gods spoke to Indra, the god of thunder: 'O giver of earthly goods, go and see who is that being that fills us with wonder.' And Indra ran towards Brahman, the Spirit Supreme, but he disappeared.

Then in the same region of the sky the god saw a lady of radiant beauty. She was Uma, divine wisdom, the daughter of the mountains of snow. 'Who is that being that fills us with wonder?' he asked.

PART 4

'He is Brahman, the Spirit Supreme', she answered. 'Rejoice in him, since through him you attained the glory of victory.'

And the gods Agni, Vayu and Indra excelled the other gods, for they were the first that came near Brahman and they first knew he was the Spirit Supreme.

And thus Indra, the god of thunder, excelled all other gods, for he came nearest to Brahman and he first knew that he was the Spirit Supreme.

Concerning whom it is said:

He is seen in Nature in the wonder of a flash of lightning. He comes to the soul in the wonder of a flash of vision. His name is Tadvanam, which translated means 'the End of love-longing'. As Tadvanam he should have adoration. All beings will love such a lover of the Lord.

Master. You asked me to explain the *Upanishad*, the sacred wisdom. The *Upanishad* has been explained to you. In truth I have been telling you the sacred teaching concerning Brahman.

KATHA UPANISHAD

PART I

VAJASRAVASA gave away all his possessions at a sacrifice; but it was out of desire for heaven.

He had a son called Nachiketas who, although he was only a boy, had a vision of faith when the offerings were given and thus he thought:

'This poor offering of cows that are too old to give milk and too weak to eat grass or drink water must lead to a world of sorrow.'

And he thought of offering himself, and said to his father: 'Father, to whom will you give me?' He asked once, and twice, and three times; and then his father answered in anger: 'I will give you to Death.'

Nachiketas. At the head of many I go, and I go in the midst of many. What may be the work of Death that today must be done through me?

Remember how the men of old passed away, and how those of days to come will also pass away: a mortal ripens like corn, and like corn is born again.

Nachiketas had to wait three nights without food in the abode of YAMA, the god of death.

A Voice. As the spirit of fire a Brahmin comes to a house: bring the offering of water, O god of Death.

How unwise is the man who does not give hospitality to a Brahmin! He loses his future hopes, his past merits, his present possessions: his sons and his all.

Death. Since you have come as a sacred guest to my abode, and you have had no hospitality for three nights, choose then three boons.

Nachiketas. May my father's anger be appeased, and may

55

he remember me and welcome me when I return to him. Let this be my first boon.

Death. By my power your father will remember you and love you as before; and when he sees you free from the jaws of death, sweet will be his sleep at night.

Nachiketas. There is no fear in heaven: old age and death are not there. The good, beyond both, rejoice in heaven, beyond hunger and thirst and sorrow.

And those in heaven attain immortality. You know, O Death, that sacred fire which leads to heaven. Explain it to me, since I have faith. Be this my second boon.

Death. I know, Nachiketas, that sacred fire which leads to heaven. Listen. That fire which is the means of attaining the infinite worlds, and is also their foundation, is hidden in the sacred place of the heart.

And Death told him of the fire of creation, the beginning of the worlds, and of the altar of the fire-sacrifice, of how many bricks it should be built and how they should be placed. Nachiketas repeated the teaching. Death was pleased and went on:

A further boon I give you today. This fire of sacrifice shall be known by your name. Take also from me this chain of many forms.

One who lights three times this sacred fire, and attains union with the Three, and performs the three holy actions, passes beyond life and death; for then he knows the god of fire, the god who knows all things, and through knowledge and adoration he attains the peace supreme.

He who, knowing the Three, builds up the altar of fire-sacrifice and performs three times the sacrifice of Nachiketas, casts off the bonds of death and, passing beyond sorrow, finds joy in the regions of heaven.

This is the fire that leads to heaven which you chose as the second gift. Men will call it the fire-sacrifice of Nachiketas. Choose now the third boon.

Nachiketas. When a man dies, this doubt arises: some say 'he is' and some say 'he is not'. Teach me the truth.

Death. Even the gods had this doubt in times of old; for mysterious is the law of life and death. Ask for another boon. Release me from this.

Nachiketas. This doubt indeed arose even to the gods, and you say, O Death, that it is difficult to understand; but no greater teacher than you can explain it, and there is no other boon so great as this.

Death. Take horses and gold and cattle and elephants; choose sons and grandsons that shall live a hundred years. Have vast expanses of land, and live as many years as you desire.

Or choose another gift that you think equal to this, and enjoy it with wealth and long life. Be a ruler of this vast earth. I will grant you all your desires.

Ask for any wishes in the world of mortals, however hard to obtain. To attend on you I will give you fair maidens with chariots and musical instruments. But ask me not, Nachiketas, the secrets of death.

Nachiketas. All these pleasures pass away, O End of all! They weaken the power of life. And indeed how short is all life! Keep thy horses and dancing and singing.

Man cannot be satisfied with wealth. Shall we enjoy wealth with you in sight? Shall we live whilst you are in power? I can only ask for the boon I have asked.

When a mortal here on earth has felt his own immortality, could he wish for a long life of pleasures, for the lust of deceitful beauty?

Solve then the doubt as to the great beyond. Grant me the gift that unveils the mystery. This is the only gift Nachiketas can ask.

PART 2 *Distinction between joy & pleasure*

Death. There is the path of joy, and there is the path of pleasure. Both attract the soul. Who follows the first comes to good; who follows pleasure reaches not the End.

The two paths lie in front of man. Pondering on them,

joy — superior word

the wise man chooses the path of joy; the fool takes the path of pleasure.

You have pondered, Nachiketas, on pleasures and you have rejected them. You have not accepted that chain of possessions wherewith men bind themselves and beneath which they sink.

There is the path of wisdom and the path of ignorance. They are far apart and lead to different ends. You are, Nachiketas, a follower of the path of wisdom: many pleasures tempt you not.

Abiding in the midst of ignorance, thinking themselves wise and learned, fools go aimlessly hither and thither, like blind led by the blind.

What lies beyond life shines not to those who are childish, or careless, or deluded by wealth. 'This is the only world: there is no other', they say; and thus they go from death to death.

Not many hear of him; and of those not many reach him. Wonderful is he who can teach about him; and wise is he who can be taught. Wonderful is he who knows him when taught.

He cannot be taught by one who has not reached him; and he cannot be reached by much thinking. The way to him is through a Teacher who has seen him: He is higher than the highest thoughts, in truth above all thought.

This sacred knowledge is not attained by reasoning; but it can be given by a true Teacher. As your purpose is steady you have found him. May I find another pupil like you!

I know that treasures pass away and that the Eternal is not reached by the transient. I have thus laid the fire of sacrifice of Nachiketas, and by burning in it the transient I have reached the Eternal.

Before your eyes have been spread, Nachiketas, the fulfilment of all desire, the dominion of the world, the eternal reward of ritual, the shore where there is no fear, the greatness of fame and boundless spaces. With strength and wisdom you have renounced them all.

When the wise rests his mind in contemplation on our God beyond time, who invisibly dwells in the mystery of things and in the heart of man, then he rises above pleasures and sorrow.

When a man has heard and has understood and, finding the essence, reaches the Inmost, then he finds joy in the Source of joy. Nachiketas is a house open for thy Atman, thy God.

Nachiketas. Tell me what you see beyond right and wrong, beyond what is done or not done, beyond past and future.

Death. I will tell you the Word that all the *Vedas* glorify, all self-sacrifice expresses, all sacred studies and holy life seek. That Word is OM.

That Word is the everlasting Brahman: that Word is the highest End. When that sacred Word is known, all longings are fulfilled.

It is the supreme means of salvation: it is the help supreme. When that great Word is known, one is great in the heaven of Brahman.

Atman, the Spirit of vision, is never born and never dies. Before him there was nothing, and he is ONE for evermore. Never-born and eternal, beyond times gone or to come, he does not die when the body dies.

If the slayer thinks that he kills, and if the slain thinks that he dies, neither knows the ways of truth. The Eternal in man cannot kill: the Eternal in man cannot die.

Concealed in the heart of all beings is the Atman, the Spirit, the Self; smaller than the smallest atom, greater than the vast spaces. The man who surrenders his human will leaves sorrows behind, and beholds the glory of the Atman by the grace of the Creator.

Resting, he wanders afar; sleeping, he goes everywhere. Who else but my Self can know that God of joy and of sorrows?

When the wise realize the omnipresent Spirit, who rests invisible in the visible and permanent in the impermanent, then they go beyond sorrow.

Not through much learning is the Atman reached, not through the intellect and sacred teaching. It is reached by the chosen of him – because they choose him. To his chosen the Atman reveals his glory.

Not even through deep knowledge can the Atman be reached, unless evil ways are abandoned, and there is rest in the senses, concentration in the mind and peace in one's heart.

Who knows in truth where he is? The majesty of his power carries away priests and warriors, and death itself is carried away.

PART 3

In the secret high place of the heart there are two beings who drink the wine of life in the world of truth. Those who know Brahman, those who keep the five sacred fires and those who light the three-fold fire of Nachiketas call them 'light' and 'shade'.

May we light the sacred fire of Nachiketas, the bridge to cross to the other shore where there is no fear, the supreme everlasting Spirit!

Know the Atman as Lord of a chariot; and the body as the chariot itself. Know that reason is the charioteer; and the mind indeed is the reins.

The horses, they say, are the senses; and their paths are the objects of sense. When the soul becomes one with the mind and the senses he is called 'one who has joys and sorrows'.

He who has not right understanding and whose mind is never steady is not the ruler of his life, like a bad driver with wild horses.

But he who has right understanding and whose mind is ever steady is the ruler of his life, like a good driver with well-trained horses.

He who has not right understanding, is careless and never pure, reaches not the End of the journey; but wanders on from death to death.

But he who has understanding, is careful and ever pure, reaches the End of the journey, from which he never returns.

The man whose chariot is driven by reason, who watches and holds the reins of his mind, reaches the End of the journey, the supreme everlasting Spirit.

Beyond the senses are their objects, and beyond the objects is the mind. Beyond the mind is pure reason, and beyond reason is the Spirit in man.

Beyond the Spirit in man is the Spirit of the universe, and beyond is Purusha, the Spirit Supreme. Nothing is beyond Purusha: He is the End of the path.

The light of the Atman, the Spirit, is invisible, concealed in all beings. It is seen by the seers of the subtle, when their vision is keen and is clear.

The wise should surrender speech in mind, mind in the knowing self, the knowing self in the Spirit of the universe, and the Spirit of the universe in the Spirit of peace.

Awake, arise! Strive for the Highest, and be in the Light! Sages say the path is narrow and difficult to tread, narrow as the edge of a razor.

The Atman is beyond sound and form, without touch and taste and perfume. It is eternal, unchangeable, and without beginning or end: indeed above reasoning. When consciousness of the Atman manifests itself, man becomes free from the jaws of death.

The wise who can learn and can teach this ancient story of Nachiketas, taught by Yama, the god of death, finds glory in the world of Brahman.

He who, filled with devotion, recites this supreme mystery at the gathering of Brahmins, or at the ceremony of the Sradha for the departed, prepares for Eternity, he prepares in truth for Eternity.

PART 4

The Creator made the senses outward-going: they go to the world of matter outside, not to the Spirit within. But a sage who sought immortality looked within himself and found his own Soul.

The foolish run after outward pleasures and fall into the snares of vast-embracing death. But the wise have found immortality, and do not seek the Eternal in things that pass away.

This by which we perceive colours and sounds, perfumes and kisses of love; by which alone we attain knowledge; by which verily we can be conscious of anything:

This in truth is That.

When the wise knows that it is through the great and omnipresent Spirit in us that we are conscious in waking or in dreaming, then he goes beyond sorrow.

When he knows the Atman, the Self, the inner life, who enjoys like a bee the sweetness of the flowers of the senses, the Lord of what was and of what will be, then he goes beyond fear:

This in truth is That.

The god of creation, who in the beginning was born from the fire of thought before the waters were; who appeared in the elements and rests, having entered the heart:

This in truth is That.

The goddess of Infinity who comes as Life-power and Nature; who was born from the elements and rests, having entered the heart:

This in truth is That.

Agni, the all-knowing god of fire, hidden in the two friction fire-sticks of the holy sacrifice, as a seed of life in the womb of a mother, who receives the morning adoration of those who follow the path of light or the path of work:

This in truth is That.

Whence the rising sun does come, and into which it sets again; wherein all the gods have their birth, and beyond which no man can go:

This in truth is That.

What is here is also there, and what is there is also here.

Who sees the many and not the ONE, wanders on from death to death.

Even by the mind this truth is to be learned: there are not many but only ONE. Who sees variety and not the unity wanders on from death to death.

The soul dwells within us, a flame the size of a thumb. When it is known as the Lord of the past and the future, then ceases all fear:

This in truth is That.

Like a flame without smoke, the size of a thumb, is the soul; the Lord of the past and the future, the same both today and tomorrow:

This in truth is That.

As water raining on a mountain-ridge runs down the rocks on all sides, so the man who only sees variety of things runs after them on all sides.

But as pure water raining on pure water becomes one and the same, so becomes, O Nachiketas, the soul of the sage who knows.

PART 5

The pure eternal Spirit dwells in the castle of eleven gates of the body. By ruling this castle, man is free from sorrows and, free from all bondage, attains liberation.

'In space he is the sun, and he is the wind and the sky; at the altar he is the priest, and the Soma wine in the jar. He dwells in men and in gods, in righteousness and in the vast heavens. He is in the earth and the waters and in the rocks of the mountains. He is Truth and Power.'

The powers of life adore that god who is in the heart, and he rules the breath of life, breathing in and breathing out.

When the ties that bind the Spirit to the body are unloosed and the Spirit is set free, what remains then?

This in truth is That.

A mortal lives not through that breath that flows in and

that flows out. The source of his life is another and this causes the breath to flow.

I will now speak to you of the mystery of the eternal Brahman; and of what happens to the soul after death.

The soul may go to the womb of a mother and thus obtain a new body. It even may go into trees or plants, according to its previous wisdom and work.

There is a Spirit who is awake in our sleep and creates the wonder of dreams. He is Brahman, the Spirit of Light, who in truth is called the Immortal. All the worlds rest on that Spirit and beyond him no one can go:

This in truth is That.

As fire, though one, takes new forms in all things that burn, the Spirit, though one, takes new forms in all things that live. He is within all, and is also outside.

As the wind, though one, takes new forms in whatever it enters, the Spirit, though one, takes new forms in all things that live. He is within all, and is also outside.

As the sun that beholds the world is untouched by earthly impurities, so the Spirit that is in all things is untouched by external sufferings.

There is one Ruler, the Spirit that is in all things, who transforms his own form into many. Only the wise who see him in their souls attain the joy eternal.

He is the Eternal among things that pass away, pure Consciousness of conscious beings, the ONE who fulfils the prayers of many. Only the wise who see him in their souls attain the peace eternal.

'This is That' – thus they realize the ineffable joy supreme. How can 'This' be known? Does he give light or does he reflect light?

There the sun shines not, nor the moon, nor the stars; lightnings shine not there and much less earthly fire. From his light all these give light, and his radiance illumines all creation.

PART 6

The Tree of Eternity has its roots in heaven above and its branches reach down to earth. It is Brahman, pure Spirit, who in truth is called the Immortal. All the worlds rest on that Spirit and beyond him no one can go:

This in truth is That.

The whole universe comes from him and his life burns through the whole universe. In his power is the majesty of thunder. Those who know him have found immortality.

From fear of him fire burns, and from fear of him the sun shines. From fear of him the clouds and the winds, and death itself, move on their way.

If one sees him in this life before the body passes away, one is free from bondage; but if not, one is born and dies again in new worlds and new creations.

Brahman is seen in a pure soul as in a mirror clear, and also in the Creator's heaven as clear as light; but in the land of shades as remembrance of dreams, and in the world of spirits as reflections in trembling waters.

When the wise man knows that the material senses come not from the Spirit, and that their waking and sleeping belong to their own nature, then he grieves no more.

Beyond the senses is the mind, and beyond mind is reason, its essence. Beyond reason is the Spirit in man, and beyond this is the Spirit of the universe, the evolver of all.

And beyond is Purusha, all-pervading, beyond definitions. When a mortal knows him, he attains liberation and reaches immortality.

His form is not in the field of vision: no one sees him with mortal eyes. He is seen by a pure heart and by a mind and thoughts that are pure. Those who know him attain life immortal.

When the five senses and the mind are still, and reason itself rests in silence, then begins the Path supreme.

This calm steadiness of the senses is called Yoga. Then

one should become watchful, because Yoga comes and goes.

Words and thoughts cannot reach him and he cannot be seen by the eye. How can he then be perceived except by him who says 'He is'?

In the faith of 'He is' his existence must be perceived, and he must be perceived in his essence. When he is perceived as 'He is', then shines forth the revelation of his essence.

When all desires that cling to the heart are surrendered, then a mortal becomes immortal, and even in this world he is one with Brahman.

When all the ties that bind the heart are unloosened, then a mortal becomes immortal. This is the sacred teaching.

One hundred and one subtle ways come from the heart. One of them rises to the crown of the head. This is the way that leads to immortality; the others lead to different ends.

Always dwelling within all beings is the Atman, the Purusha, the Self, a little flame in the heart. Let one with steadiness withdraw him from the body even as an inner stem is withdrawn from its sheath. Know this pure immortal light; know in truth this pure immortal light.

And Nachiketas learnt the supreme wisdom taught by the god of after-life, and he learnt the whole teaching of inner-union, of Yoga. Then he reached Brahman, the Spirit Supreme, and became immortal and pure. So in truth will anyone who knows his Atman, his higher Self.

ॐ

PRASNA UPANISHAD

FIRST QUESTION

SUKESA BHARADVAJA, Saibya Satyakama, Sauryayani Gargya, Kausalya Asvalayana, Bhargava Vaidarbhi and Kabandhi Katyayana were students filled with devotion for Brahman, the Supreme Spirit; their minds rested on Brahman, and they were in search of the Highest Brahman. Once they said: 'The holy Pippalada can explain all the sacred teaching'; and, thus thinking, they approached him, bringing as a sign of reverence fuel for the sacred fire.

The sage said to them: Remain another year in steadiness, purity and faith. Ask then anything you desire and, if I know, I will tell you all.

When the time came, Kabandhi Katyayana approached the sage and said: Master, whence came all created beings?

The sage replied: In the beginning, the Creator longed for the joy of creation. He remained in meditation, and then came Rayi, matter, and Prana, life. 'These two', thought he, 'will produce beings for me'.

The sun is life and the moon is matter. All that has form, solid or subtle, is matter: therefore form is matter.

When the rising morning sun enters the eastern skies, then he bathes in his light all life that is in the East. And then the South and the West and the North and all the sky are illumined by that light that gives life to all that lives.

Thus rises the sun as fire, as life in its infinite variety. It was said in a verse of the *Rig Veda*:

'The sun is rising in golden radiance! The sun of a thousand rays in a hundred regions abiding; the god omniscient, the aim of all prayers; the light and fire supreme, the infinite life of all beings.'

The Lord of Creation is in truth the time of the year.

This has two paths: the way of the South and the way of the North. Those who worship thinking, 'We have done sacrifices and pious works', attain only the regions of the moon and return to life and death. That is why those sages who desire children and the life of the family follow the path of the South. This is the path that leads to the ancestors.

But those who in search of the inner Spirit follow the spiritual path of the North with steadiness, purity, faith, and wisdom attain the regions of the sun. And there is the ocean of life, the refuge supreme, the land of immortality where there is no fear. From there they do not return again: it is the end of the journey. There is a verse of the *Rig Veda* that says:

'Some speak of a Father who sends rain from the heaven of the North, resting on the seasons and showing himself in twelve ways. Others speak of a sage in the heaven of the South with a chariot of seven wheels and six spokes.'

The day and night are the Lord of Creation. Day is life and night is matter. Those who join in love by day waste life; but they follow the good path, those who join in love by night.

The dark fortnight is indeed matter, and the bright fortnight is life. Some sages perform their rituals in the bright fortnight; but some in the time of darkness.

Food is in truth the Lord of Creation. From food seed is produced and from this beings are born.

Those who obey the Law of the Lord of Creation, they in turn become creators and like him produce a pair. They attain the pale regions of the moon.

But those in whom there is no deceit, untruth or bad faith, who live in steadiness, purity, and truth, theirs are the radiant regions of the sun.

SECOND QUESTION

Then Bhargava Vaidarbhi asked: Master, what are the powers that keep the union of a being, how many keep burning the lamps of life, and which amongst them is supreme?

The sage replied: The powers are space, air, fire, water, and earth; and voice, mind, the eye, and the ear. These powers light the lamps of life and say: 'We keep the union of this being and we are its foundation'.

But Life, the power supreme, said to them: 'Do not fall into delusion. It is I who, in my fivefold division, keep the union of this being and I am its foundation.' But they believed him not.

Life was offended and rose aloft to leave the body, and all the powers of life had to rise and, Life coming again to rest, all the powers had to rest. As when a queen-bee arises, all the bees with her arise, and when she comes to rest again, then all again come to rest, even so it happened to the powers of the voice, the mind, the eye, and the ear. The powers then understood and sang in joy this song of life:

'Life is the fire that burns and is the sun that gives light. Life is the wind and the rain and the thunder in the sky. Life is matter and is earth, what is and what is not, and what beyond is in Eternity.

On Life all things are resting, as spokes in the centre of a wheel. On Life are resting the *Vedas* and prayers and warriors and priests.

To thee, resting with thy powers, O Life, all beings offer adoration. As Lord of Creation thou movest in the womb of the mother, thence to be reborn.

Thou art the chief bearer of gifts to the gods, the first offering made to the departed; thou art the poetry of the seers, the truth of ancient sages.

Thou art Rudra, the god of protection; thou art Indra in thy radiance, O Life. As the sun that wanders in heaven, thou art Lord of all heavenly lights.

When the rain pours down from heaven, O Life, all thy creatures rejoice and they say: 'Food for us shall be in abundance'.

Thou art pure, O Life, supreme seer, lord and consumer

of all. We, the givers of what thou enjoyest, thou, our father, the breath of all life.

Be favourable unto us, O Life, with that invisible form of thine which is in the voice, the eye, and the ear, and which lives in the mind. Go not from us.

In thy power is all this world and even the third most sacred heaven. As a mother her child, protect us, O Life: give us glory and give us wisdom.'

THIRD QUESTION

Then Kausalya Asvalayana asked: Master, this life, whence does it arise? How does it come to this body? How, after diffusing itself, does it abide here? How does it leave the body? How does it sustain the universe without and the universe within?

The sage replied: Great are the questions you ask from me, but you are a great lover of Brahman: I will answer.

Life comes from the Spirit. Even as a man casts a shadow, so the Spirit casts the shadow of life, and, as a shadow of former lives, a new life comes to this body.

As when a ruler commands his officials and appoints them cities to be ruled, in his name, even so Prana, the power of life, rules the other living powers of the body.

Apana rules its lower regions. Prana itself lives in the eye and the ear and moves through the nose and the mouth. Samana rules the middle regions, and distributes the life-giving offering of food. From Samana come the seven flames.

In the heart dwells the Atman, the Self. It is the centre of a hundred and one little channels. From each one of them come a hundred channels more. Seventy-two thousand smaller channels branch from each one of these. In all these millions of little channels moves the power of Vyana.

Rising by one of them, the living power of Udana leads to the heaven of purity by good actions, to the hell of evil by evil actions, and if by both again to this land of man.

The sun is Prana, the life of this universe, and he rises

giving joy to the life in human eyes. The divinity of the earth rules the lower regions of Apana. Between the sun and the earth there is space or Samana. Air is Vyana.

Fire is Udana. When that fire of life is gone, senses are absorbed in mind, and man comes to life again. His last thoughts lead him to Prana and, accompanied by the living fire of Udana and led by Atman, the Spirit himself, he goes to the regions deserved and desired in imagination.

He who thus knows the meaning of life, his off-spring never dies and attains life everlasting. There is a verse that says:

'He who knows the rising of life and how it comes to the body, how it abides there in its fivefold division, and knows its relation to the inner Spirit, enjoys eternal life, in truth enjoys eternal life.'

FOURTH QUESTION

Then Sauryayani Gargya asked: Master, how many powers sleep in man and how many remain awake? Who is that Spirit that beholds the wonder of dreams? Who enjoys the mystery of sleep with no dreams? Who is that Spirit on whom all the others find rest?

The sage replied: As when, before darkness falls, the rays of the setting sun seem all to become one in its circle of light, though at the hour of sunrise they all spread out again, even so all the powers of the senses become one in the higher power of the mind. Then a person does not see, hear, smell, taste or touch; does not speak, receive or give, move, or enjoy joys of love. Then people say 'he sleeps'.

But in the city of the body the fires of life are burning: they sleep not. Apana is like the sacred home-fire for ever kept burning from father to son. Vyana is like the fire of the South for offerings to the ancestors. Prana is like the fire of the East lit up by the home-fire.

Samana is like the Hotri priest evenly distributing the two offerings of expiration and inspiration. The mind is the performer of the sacrifice; and Udana is its fruit, since every day it takes the mind in sleep to Brahman, the Almighty.

And in dreams the mind beholds its own immensity. What has been seen is seen again, and what has been heard is heard again. What has been felt in different places or faraway regions returns to the mind again. Seen and unseen, heard and unheard, felt and not felt, the mind sees all, since the mind is all.

But when the mind is overcome by its own radiance, then dreams are no longer seen: joy and peace come to the body.

Even as birds, O beloved, return to their tree for rest, thus all things find their rest in Atman, the Supreme Spirit.

All things find their final peace in their inmost Self, the Spirit: earth, water, fire, air, space, and their invisible elements; sight, hearing, smell, taste, touch, and their various fields of sense; voice, hands, and all powers of action mind, reason, the sense of 'I', thought, inner light, and their objects; and even life and all that life sustains.

It is the Spirit of man who sees, hears, feels perfumes, touches and tastes, thinks and acts and has all consciousness. And the Spirit of man finds peace in the Spirit Supreme and Eternal.

He who knows, O my son, that Eternal Spirit, incorporeal and shadowless, luminous and everlasting, attains that Eternal Spirit. He knows the All and becomes the All. A verse there is that says:

'He who knows, O my beloved, that Eternal Spirit wherein consciousness and the senses, the powers of life and the elements find final peace, knows the All and has gone into the All.'

FIFTH QUESTION

Then Saibya Satyakama asked: Master, that man who until the end of his life rests on OM his meditation, where does he go after life?

The sage replied: The Word OM, O Satyakama, is the transcendent and the immanent Brahman, the Spirit Supreme. With the help of this sacred Word the wise attains the one or the other.

OM, or AUM, has three sounds. He who rests on the first his meditation is illumined thereby and after death returns speedily to this world of men led by the harmonies of the *Rig Veda*. Remaining here in steadiness, purity, and truth he attains greatness.

And if he rests his mind in meditation on the first two sounds, he is led by the harmonies of the *Yajur Veda* to the regions of the moon. After enjoying their heavenly joys, he returns to earth again.

But if, with the three sounds of the eternal OM, he places his mind in meditation upon the Supreme Spirit, he comes to the regions of light of the sun. There he becomes free from all evil, even as a snake sheds its old skin, and with the harmonies of the *Sama Veda* he goes to the heaven of Brahma wherefrom he can behold the Spirit that dwells in the city of the human body and which is above the highest life. There are two verses that say:

'The three sounds not in union lead again to life that dies; but the wise who merge them into a harmony of union in outer, inner and middle actions becomes steady: he trembles no more.'

With the harmonies of the *Rig Veda* unto this world of man, and with those of the *Yajur Veda* to the middle heavenly regions; but, with the help of OM, the sage goes to those regions that the seers know in the harmonies of the *Sama Veda*. There he finds the peace of the Supreme Spirit where there is no dissolution or death and where there is no fear.

SIXTH QUESTION

Then Sukesa Bharadvaja said: Master, Prince Hiranyanabha Kausalya came once to me and asked this question: 'Do you know the Spirit of sixteen forms?' 'I know him not',

I answered the young prince. 'If I knew him, how could I say that I knew him not? For he who speaks untruth withers like a tree to the roots: I will not speak untruth.' The prince became silent and, mounting his chariot, departed. And now I ask you. Where is that Spirit?

The sage replied: O my son, the Spirit in whom sixteen forms arise is here within this body.

The Spirit thought: 'In whose going out shall I go out, and in whose staying shall I stay?'

And he created life, and from life faith and space and air, light, water, and earth, the senses and the mind. He created food and from food strength, austerity, sacred poems, holy actions, and even the worlds. And in the worlds, name was created.

As when rivers flowing towards the ocean find there final peace, their name and form disappear, and people speak only of the ocean, even so the sixteen forms of the seer of all flow towards the Spirit and find there final peace, their name and form disappear and people speak only of Spirit. There is a verse that says:

'These forms in him find rest like spokes in the centre of a wheel. Know ye the Spirit that should be known that death may afflict you not.'

Then the sage said to the disciples: Thus far I know the Supreme Spirit. There is nothing beyond.

Bowing to him in adoration, the disciples said: You are in truth our father who has saved us from ignorance and has led us to the shore beyond.

Adoration to the supreme seers! Adoration to the supreme seers!

MUNDAKA UPANISHAD

PART I

CHAPTER I

BRAHMA was before the gods were, the Creator of all, the Guardian of the Universe. The vision of Brahman, the foundation of all wisdom, he gave in revelation to his first-born son Atharvan.

That vision and wisdom of Brahman given to Atharvan, he in olden times revealed to Angira. And Angira gave it to Satyavaha, who in succession revealed it to Angiras.

Now there was a man whose name was Saunaka, owner of a great household, who, approaching one day Angiras with reverence, asked him this question: 'Master, what is that which, when known, all is known?' The Master replied: Sages say that there are two kinds of wisdom, the higher and the lower.

The lower wisdom is in the four sacred *Vedas*, and in the six kinds of knowledge that help to know, to sing, and to use the *Vedas*: definition and grammar, pronunciation and poetry, ritual and the signs of heaven. But the higher wisdom is that which leads to the Eternal.

He is beyond thought and invisible, beyond family and colour. He has neither eyes nor ears; he has neither hands nor feet. He is everlasting and omnipresent, infinite in the great and infinite in the small. He is the Eternal whom the sages see as the source of all creation.

Even as a spider sends forth and draws in its thread, even as plants arise from the earth and hairs from the body of man, even so the whole creation arises from the Eternal.

By *Tapas*, the power of meditation, Brahman attains expansion and then comes primeval matter. And from this

75

comes life and mind, the elements and the worlds and the immortality of ritual action.

From that Spirit who knows all and sees all, whose *Tapas* is pure vision, from him comes Brahma, the creator, name and form and primal matter.

CHAPTER 2

This is the truth: The actions of devotion that sages heard in sacred verses were told in many ways in the three *Vedas*. Perform them always, O lovers of the true: they are your path of holy action in this world.

When the flames of the sacred fire are rising, place then in faith the sacred offerings.

If at the sacred fire of Agnihotra no heed is taken of the new moon, or of the full moon, or of the seasons of the year, or of the first fruits of spring; if no guests are present, if the offering of the sacrifice is left undone, or not done according to rule, or the offering to all the gods is forgotten, then the offerer does not attain the reward of the seven worlds.

The dancing flames of the sacred fire are seven: the black, the terrific, that which is swift as the mind, that which is dark with smoke, the deep red, the spark-blazing and the luminous omniformed flame.

If a man begins his sacrifice when the flames are luminous, and considers for the offerings the signs of heaven, then the holy offerings lead him on the rays of the sun where the Lord of all gods has his high dwelling.

And when on the rays of sunlight the radiant offerings raise him, then they glorify him in words of melody: 'Welcome', they say, 'welcome here. Enjoy the heaven of Brahma won by pure holy actions.'

But unsafe are the boats of sacrifice to go to the farthest shore; unsafe are the eighteen books where the lower actions are explained. The unwise who praise them as the highest end go to old age and death again.

Abiding in the midst of ignorance, but thinking themselves wise and learned, fools aimlessly go hither and thither, like blind led by the blind.

Wandering in the paths of unwisdom, 'We have attained the end of life', think the foolish. Clouds of passion conceal to them the beyond, and sad is their fall when the reward of their pious actions has been enjoyed.

Imagining religious ritual and gifts of charity as the final good, the unwise see not the Path supreme. Indeed they have in high heaven the reward of their pious actions; but thence they fall and come to earth or even down to lower regions.

But those who in purity and faith live in the solitude of the forest, who have wisdom and peace and long not for earthly possessions, those in radiant purity pass through the gates of the sun to the dwelling-place supreme where the Spirit is in Eternity.

Beholding the worlds of creation, let the lover of God attain renunciation: what is above creation cannot be attained by action. In his longing for divine wisdom, let him go with reverence to a Teacher, in whom live the sacred words and whose soul has peace in Brahman.

To a pupil who comes with mind and senses in peace the Teacher gives the vision of Brahman, of the Spirit of truth and eternity.

PART 2

CHAPTER I

This is the truth: As from a fire aflame thousands of sparks come forth, even so from the Creator an infinity of beings have life and to him return again.

But the spirit of light above form, never-born, within all, outside all, is in radiance above life and mind, and beyond this creation's Creator.

From him comes all life and mind, and the senses of all life. From him comes space and light, air and fire and water, and this earth that holds us all.

The head of his body is fire, and his eyes the sun and the moon; his ears, the regions of heaven, and the sacred *Vedas* his word. His breath is the wind that blows, and this whole universe is his heart. This earth is his footstool. He is the Spirit that is in all things.

From him comes the sun, and the source of all fire is the sun.

From him comes the moon, and from this comes the rain and all herbs that grow upon earth. And man comes from him, and man unto woman gives seed; and thus an infinity of beings come from the Spirit supreme.

The verses of the *Rig Veda* and songs of the *Sama Veda*, prayers of the *Yajur Veda* and rites of initiation, sacrifices and offerings and gifts, the offerer of the sacrifice, the year and the worlds purified by the light from the sun and the moon, all come from the Spirit.

From him the oceans and mountains; and all rivers come from him. And all herbs and the essence of all whereby the Inner Spirit dwells with the elements: all come from him.

The spirit in truth is all: action, and the power of Tapas, and Brahma the creator, and immortality. He who knows him dwelling in the secret place of the heart cuts asunder the bonds of ignorance even in this human life.

CHAPTER 2

Radiant in his light, yet invisible in the secret place of the heart, the Spirit is the supreme abode wherein dwells all that moves and breathes and sees. Know him as all that is, and all that is not, the end of love-longing beyond understanding, the highest in all beings.

He is self-luminous and more subtle than the smallest; but in him rest all the worlds and their beings. He is the everlasting Brahman, and he is life and word and mind. He is truth and life immortal. He is the goal to be aimed at: attain that goal, O my son!

Take the great bow of the *Upanishads* and place in it an arrow sharp with devotion. Draw the bow with concentration on him and hit the centre of the mark, the same everlasting Spirit.

The bow is the sacred OM, and the arrow is our own soul. Brahman is the mark of the arrow, the aim of the soul. Even as an arrow becomes one with its mark, let the watchful soul be one in him.

In him are woven the sky and the earth and all the regions of the air, and in him rest the mind and all the powers of life. Know him as the ONE and leave aside all other words. He is the bridge of immortality.

Where all the subtle channels of the body meet, like spokes in the centre of a wheel, there he moves in the heart and transforms his one form unto many. Upon OM, Atman, your Self, place your meditation. Glory unto you in your far-away journey beyond darkness!

He who knows all and sees all, and whose glory the universe shows, dwells as the Spirit of the divine city of Brahman in the region of the human heart. He becomes mind and drives on the body and life, draws power from food and finds peace in the heart. There the wise find him as joy and light and life eternal.

And when he is seen in his immanence and transcendence, then the ties that have bound the heart are unloosened, the doubts of the mind vanish, and the law of Karma works no more.

In the supreme golden chamber is Brahman indivisible and pure. He is the radiant light of all lights, and this knows he who knows Brahman.

There the sun shines not, nor the moon, nor the stars; lightnings shine not there and much less earthly fire. From his light all these give light; and his radiance illumines all creation.

Far spreading before and behind and right and left, and above and below, is Brahman, the Spirit eternal. In truth Brahman is all.

PART 3

CHAPTER I

There are two birds, two sweet friends, who dwell on the self-same tree. The one eats the fruits thereof, and the other looks on in silence.

The first is the human soul who, resting on that tree, though active, feels sad in his unwisdom. But on beholding the power and glory of the higher Spirit, he becomes free from sorrow.

When the wise seer beholds in golden glory the Lord, the Spirit, the Creator of the god of creation, then he leaves good and evil behind and in purity he goes to the unity supreme.

In silent wonder the wise see him as the life flaming in all creation. This is the greatest seer of Brahman, who, doing all his work as holy work, in God, in Atman, in the Self, finds all his peace and joy.

This Atman is attained by truth and *tapas* whence come true wisdom and chastity. The wise who strive and who are pure see him within the body in his pure glory and light.

Truth obtains victory, not untruth. Truth is the way that leads to the regions of light. Sages travel therein free from desires and reach the supreme abode of Truth.

He is immeasurable in his light and beyond all thought, and yet he shines smaller than the smallest. Far, far away is he, and yet he is very near, resting in the inmost chamber of the heart.

He cannot be seen by the eye, and words cannot reveal him. He cannot be reached by the senses, or by austerity or sacred actions. By the grace of wisdom and purity of mind, he can be seen indivisible in the silence of contemplation.

This invisible Atman can be seen by the mind, wherein the five senses are resting. All mind is woven with the senses; but in a pure mind shines the light of the Self.

Whatever regions the pure in heart may see in his mind,

whatever desires he may have in his heart, he attains those regions and wins his desires: let one who wishes for success reverence the seers of the Spirit.

CHAPTER 2

Then he knows the supreme dwelling of Brahman wherein the whole universe shines in radiance. The wise who, free from desires, adore the Spirit pass beyond the seed of life in death.

A man whose mind wanders among desires, and is longing for objects of desire, goes again to life and death according to his desires. But he who possesses the End of all longing, and whose self has found fulfilment, even in this life his desires will fade away.

Not through much learning is the Atman reached, not through the intellect or sacred teaching. He is reached by the chosen of him. To his chosen the Atman reveals his glory.

The Atman is not reached by the weak, or the careless, or those who practise wrong austerity; but the wise who strive in the right way lead their soul into the dwelling of Brahman.

Having reached that place supreme, the seers find joy in wisdom, their souls have fulfilment, their passions have gone, they have peace. Filled with devotion, they have found the Spirit in all and go into the All.

Those ascetics who know well the meaning of the *Vedanta*, whose minds are pure by renunciation, at the hour of departing find freedom in the regions of Brahman, and attain the supreme everlasting life.

The fifteen forms return to their sources and the senses to their divinities. Actions and the self and his knowledge go into the Supreme everlasting.

As rivers flowing into the ocean find their final peace and their name and form disappear, even so the wise become free from name and form and enter into the radiance of the Supreme Spirit who is greater than all greatness.

In truth who knows God becomes God.

MANDUKYA UPANISHAD

OM. This eternal Word is all: what was, what is and what shall be, and what beyond is in eternity. All is OM.

Brahman is all and Atman is Brahman. Atman, the Self, has four conditions.

The first condition is the waking life of outward-moving consciousness, enjoying the seven outer gross elements.

The second condition is the dreaming life of inner-moving consciousness, enjoying the seven subtle inner elements in its own light and solitude.

The third condition is the sleeping life of silent consciousness when a person has no desires and beholds no dreams. That condition of deep sleep is one of oneness, a mass of silent consciousness made of peace and enjoying peace.

This silent consciousness is all-powerful, all-knowing, the inner ruler, the source of all, the beginning and end of all beings.

The fourth condition is Atman in his own pure state: the awakened life of supreme consciousness. It is neither outer nor inner consciousness, neither semi-consciousness, nor sleeping-consciousness, neither consciousness nor unconsciousness. He is Atman, the Spirit himself, that cannot be seen or touched, that is above all distinction, beyond thought and ineffable. In the union with him is the supreme proof of his reality. He is the end of evolution and non-duality. He is peace and love.

This Atman is the eternal Word OM. Its three sounds, A, U, and M, are the first three states of consciousness, and these three states are the three sounds.

The first sound A is the first state of waking consciousness, common to all men. It is found in the words *Apti*, 'attaining', and *Adimatvam*, 'being first'. Who knows this

The life of man⁸³ is divided between waking, dreaming, sleep attains in truth all his desires, and in all things becomes first.

The second sound U is the second state of dreaming consciousness. It is found in the words *Utkarsha*, 'uprising', and *Ubhayatvam*, 'bothness'. Who knows this raises the tradition of knowledge and attains equilibrium. In his family is never born any one who knows not Brahman.

The third sound M is the third state of sleeping consciousness. It is found in the words *Miti*, 'measure', and in the root *Mi*, 'to end', that gives *Apiti*, 'final end'. Who knows this measures all with his mind and attains the final End.

The word OM as one sound is the fourth state of supreme consciousness. It is beyond the senses and is the end of evolution. It is non-duality and love. He goes with his self to the supreme Self who knows this, who knows this.

SVETASVATARA UPANISHAD

PART I

THE lovers of Brahman ask:

What is the source of this universe? What is Brahman? From where do we come? By what power do we live? Where do we find rest? Who rules over our joys and sorrows, O seers of Brahman?

Shall we think of time, or of the own nature of things, or of a law of necessity, or of chance, or of the elements, or of the power of creation of woman or man? Not a union of these, for above them is a soul who thinks. But our soul is under the power of pleasure and pain!

By the Yoga of meditation and contemplation the wise saw the power of God, hidden in his own creation. It is he who rules over all the sources of this universe, from time to the soul of man.

And they saw the Wheel of his power made of one circle, three layers, sixteen parts, fifty spokes, twenty counterspokes, six groups of eight, three paths, one rope of innumerable strands, and the great illusion:

'Three layers' – the three constituents of nature: light, fire and darkness; 'sixteen parts or segments of the rim of the Wheel' – the five elements, five means to know, five means to do, and the mind; 'fifty spokes' – fifty states of consciousness as taught in the Sankhya wisdom: five kinds of error, twenty-eight of weakness, nine of joy and eight of achievement; 'twenty counterspokes' – ten senses and their ten objects; 'six groups of eight' – forms of nature, constituents of the body, powers of Yoga, modes of feeling, gods, and virtues; 'three paths' – the Yoga of light, of love, and of life; 'one rope of innumerable strands – desire of innumerable forms; 'the great illusion' – the illusion which sees the ONE as two.

They also saw the river of life impetuously rushing with the five streams of sense-feelings which come from five sources, the five elements. Its waves are moved by five breathing winds, and its origin is a fivefold fountain of consciousness. This river has five whirlpools, and the violent waves of five sorrows. It has five stages of pain and five dangerous windings and turnings.

In this vast Wheel of creation wherein all things live and die, wanders round the human soul like a swan in restless flying, and she thinks that God is afar. But when the love of God comes down upon her, then she finds her own immortal life.

Exalted in songs has been Brahman. In him are God and the world and the soul, and he is the imperishable supporter of all. When the seers of Brahman see him in all creation, they find peace in Brahman and are free from all sorrows.

God upholds the oneness of this universe: the seen and the unseen, the transient and the eternal. The soul of man is bound by pleasure and pain; but when she sees God she is free from all fetters.

There is the soul of man with wisdom and unwisdom, power and powerlessness; there is nature, Prakriti, which is creation for the sake of the soul; and there is God, infinite, omnipresent, who watches the work of creation. When a man knows the three he knows Brahman.

Matter in time passes away, but God is for ever in Eternity, and he rules both matter and soul. By meditation on him, by contemplation of him, and by communion with him, there comes in the end the destruction of earthly delusion.

When a man knows God, he is free: his sorrows have an end, and birth and death are no more. When in inner union he is beyond the world of the body, then the third world, the world of the Spirit, is found, where the power of the All is, and man has all: for he is one with the ONE.

Know that Brahman is for ever in thee, and nothing higher is there to be known. When one sees God and the world and the soul, one sees the Three: one sees Brahman.

Even as fire is not seen in wood and yet by power it comes to light as fire, so Brahman in the universe and in the soul is revealed by the power of OM.

The soul is the wood below that can burn and be fire, and OM is the whirling friction-rod above. Prayer is the power that makes OM turn round and then the mystery of God comes to light.

God is found in the soul when sought with truth and self-sacrifice, as fire is found in wood, water in hidden springs, cream in milk, and oil in the oil-fruit.

There is a Spirit who is hidden in all things, as cream is hidden in milk, and who is the source of self-knowledge and self-sacrifice. This is Brahman, the Spirit Supreme. This is Brahman, the Spirit Supreme.

PART 2

Savitri, the god of inspiration, sent the mind and its powers to find truth. He saw the light of the god of fire and spread it over the earth.

By the grace of god Savitri, our mind is one with him and we strive with all our power for light.

Savitri gives life to our souls and then they shine in great light. He makes our mind and its powers one and leads our thoughts to heaven.

The seers of the god who sees all keep their mind and their thoughts in oneness. They sing the glory of god Savitri who has given every man his work.

I sing the songs of olden times with adoration: may my own songs follow the path of the sun. Let all the children of immortality hear me, even those who are in the highest heaven.

Where the fire of the Spirit burns, where the wind of the Spirit blows, where the Soma-wine of the Spirit overflows, there a new soul is born.

Inspired then by Savitri let us find joy in the prayers of

olden times: for if we make them our rock we shall be made pure of past sins.

With upright body, head, and neck lead the mind and its powers into thy heart; and the OM of Brahman will then be thy boat with which to cross the rivers of fear.

And when the body is in silent steadiness, breathe rhythmically through the nostrils with a peaceful ebbing and flowing of breath. The chariot of the mind is drawn by wild horses, and those wild horses have to be tamed.

Find a quiet retreat for the practice of Yoga, sheltered from the wind, level and clean, free from rubbish, smouldering fires, and ugliness, and where the sound of waters and the beauty of the place help thought and contemplation.

These are the imaginary forms that appear before the final vision of Brahman: a mist, a smoke, and a sun; a wind, fire-flies, and a fire; lightnings, a clear crystal, and a moon.

When the Yogi has full power over his body composed of the elements of earth, water, fire, air, and ether, then he obtains a new body of spiritual fire which is beyond illness, old age, and death.

The first fruits of the practice of Yoga are: health, little waste matter, and a clear complexion; lightness of the body, a pleasant scent, and a sweet voice; and an absence of greedy desires.

Even as a mirror of gold, covered by dust, when cleaned well shines again in full splendour, when a man has seen the Truth of the Spirit he is one with him, the aim of his life is fulfilled and he is ever beyond sorrow.

Then the soul of man becomes a lamp by which he finds the Truth of Brahman. Then he sees God, pure, never-born, everlasting; and when he sees God he is free from all bondage.

This is the God whose light illumines all creation, the Creator of all from the beginning. He was, he is and for ever he shall be. He is in all and he sees all.

Glory be to that God who is in the fire, who is in the waters, who is in plants and in trees, who is in all things in this vast creation. Unto that Spirit be glory and glory.

PART 3

There is ONE in whose hands is the net of Maya, who rules with his power, who rules all the worlds with his power. He is the same at the time of creation and at the time of dissolution. Those who know him attain immortality.

He is Rudra, he alone is the ONE who governs the worlds with his power. He watches over all beings and rules over their creation and their destruction.

His eyes and mouths are everywhere, his arms and feet are everywhere. He is God who made heaven and earth, who gave man his arms and who gave to the birds their wings.

May Rudra, the seer of Eternity, who gave to the gods their birth and their glory, who keeps all things under his protection, and who in the beginning created the Golden Seed, grant us the grace of pure vision.

Come down to us, Rudra, who art in the high mountains. Come and let the light of thy face, free from fear and evil, shine upon us. Come to us with thy love.

Let not the arrow in thy hand hurt man or any living being: let it be an arrow of love.

Greater than all is Brahman, the Supreme, the Infinite. He dwells in the mystery of all beings according to their forms in nature. Those who know him who knows all, and in whose glory all things are, attain immortality.

I know the Spirit supreme, radiant like the sun beyond darkness. He who knows him goes beyond death, for he is the only path to life immortal.

His infinity is beyond what is great or small, and greater than him there is nothing. Like a tree everlasting he stands in the centre of heaven, and his radiance illumines all creation.

Those who know him who is greater than all, beyond form and beyond pain, attain immortality: those who know not go to the worlds of sorrow.

All this universe is in the glory of God, of Siva the god of love. The heads and faces of men are his own and he is in the hearts of all.

He is indeed the Lord supreme whose grace moves the hearts of men. He leads us unto his own joy and to the glory of his light.

He is the inmost soul of all, which like a little flame the size of a thumb is hidden in the hearts of men. He is the master of wisdom ever reached by thought and love. He is the immortality of those who know him.

He has innumerable heads and eyes and feet, and his vastness enfolds the universe, and even a measure of ten beyond.

God is in truth the whole universe: what was, what is, and what beyond shall ever be. He is the god of life immortal, and of all life that lives by food.

His hands and feet are everywhere, he has heads and mouths everywhere: he sees all, he hears all. He is in all and he is.

The Light of consciousness comes to him through infinite powers of perception, and yet he is above these powers. He is God, the ruler of all, the infinite refuge of all.

The wandering swan of the soul dwells in the castle of nine gates of the body and flies away to enjoy the outer world. He is the master of the universe: of all that moves and of all that moves not.

Without hands he holds all things, without feet he runs everywhere. Without eyes he sees all things, without ears all things he hears. He knows all, but no one knows him, the Spirit before the beginning, the Spirit Supreme everlasting.

Concealed in the heart of all beings lies the Atman, the Spirit, the Self; smaller than the smallest atom, greater than the greatest spaces. When by the grace of God man sees the glory of God, he sees him beyond the world of desire and then sorrows are left behind.

I know that Spirit whose infinity is in all, who is ever one beyond time. I know the Spirit whom the lovers of Brahman call eternal, beyond the birth and rebirth of life.

PART 4

May God, who in the mystery of his vision and power transforms his white radiance into his many-coloured creation, from whom all things come and into whom they all return, grant us the grace of pure vision.

He is the sun, the moon, and the stars. He is the fire, the waters, and the wind. He is Brahma the creator of all, and Prajapati, the Lord of creation.

Thou this boy, and thou this maiden; Thou this man, and thou this woman; Thou art this old man who supports himself on a staff; Thou the God who appears in forms infinite.

Thou the blue bird and thou the green bird; Thou the cloud that conceals the lightning and thou the seasons and the oceans. Beyond beginning, thou art in thy infinity, and all the worlds had their beginning in thee.

There is nature, never-born, who with her three elements – light, fire, and darkness – creates all things in nature. There is the never-born soul of man bound by the pleasures of nature; and there is the Spirit of man, never-born, who has left pleasures behind in the joy of the Beyond.

There are two birds, two sweet friends, who dwell on the self-same tree. The one eats the fruits thereof, and the other looks on in silence.

The first is the human soul who, resting on that tree, though active, feels sad in his unwisdom. But on beholding the power and the glory of the higher Spirit, he becomes free from sorrow.

Of what use is the *Rig Veda* to one who does not know the Spirit from whom the *Rig Veda* comes, and in whom all things abide? For only those who have found him have found peace.

For all the sacred books, all holy sacrifice and ritual and prayers, all the words of the *Vedas*, and the whole past and present and future, come from the Spirit. With Maya, his power of wonder, he made all things, and by Maya the human soul is bound.

Know therefore that nature is Maya, but that God is the ruler of Maya; and that all beings in our universe are parts of his infinite splendour.

He rules over the sources of creation. From him comes the universe and unto him it returns. He is the Lord, the giver of blessings, the one God of our adoration, in whom there is perfect peace.

May Rudra, the seer of Eternity, who gave to the gods their birth and their glory, who keeps all things under his protection, and who in the beginning saw the Golden Seed, grant us the grace of pure vision.

Who is the God to whom we shall offer adoration? The God of gods, in whose glory the worlds are, and who rules this world of man and all living beings.

He is the God of forms infinite in whose glory all things are, smaller than the smallest atom, and yet the Creator of all, everliving in the mystery of his creation. In the vision of this God of love there is everlasting peace.

He is the Lord of all who, hidden in the heart of things, watches over the world of time. The gods and the seers of Brahman are one with him; and when a man knows him he cuts the bonds of death.

When one knows God who is hidden in the heart of all things, even as cream is hidden in milk, and in whose glory all things are, he is free from all bondage.

This is the God whose work is all the worlds, the supreme Soul who dwells for ever in the hearts of men. Those who know him through their hearts and their minds become immortal.

There is a region beyond darkness where there is neither day nor night, nor what is, nor what is not. Only Siva, the god of love, is there. It is the region of the glorious splendour of God from whom came the light of the sun, and from whom the ancient wisdom came in the beginning.

The mind cannot grasp him above, or below, or in the space in between. With whom shall we compare him whose glory is the whole universe?

Far beyond the range of vision, he cannot be seen by mortal eyes; but he can be known by the heart and the mind, and those who know him attain immortality.

A man comes to thee in fearful wonder and says: 'Thou art God who never was born. Let thy face, Rudra, shine upon me, and let thy love be my eternal protection.

'Hurt not my child, nor the child of my child; hurt not my life, my horses, or my cows. Kill not in anger our brave men, for we ever come to thee with adorations.'

PART 5

Two things are hidden in the mystery of infinity of Brahman: knowledge and ignorance. Ignorance passes away and knowledge is immortal; but Brahman is in Eternity above ignorance and knowledge.

He is the ONE in whose power are the many sources of creation, and the root and the flower of all things. The Golden Seed, the Creator, was in his mind in the beginning; and he saw him born when time began.

He is God who spreads the net of transmigration and then withdraws it in the field of life. He is the Lord who created the lords of creation, the supreme Soul who rules over all.

Even as the radiance of the sun shines everywhere in space, so does the glory of God rule over all his creation.

In the unfolding of his own nature he makes all things blossom into flower and fruit. He gives to them all their fragrance and colour. He, the ONE, the only God who rules the universe.

There is a Spirit hidden in the mystery of the *Upanishads* and the *Vedas*; and Brahma, the god of creation, owns him as his own Creator. It is the Spirit of God, seen by gods and seers of olden times who, when one with him, became immortal.

When a man is bound by the three powers of nature, he works for a selfish reward and in time he has his reward. His soul then becomes the many forms of the three powers, strays along the three paths, and wanders on through life and death.

The soul is like the sun in splendour. When it becomes one with the self-conscious 'I am' and its desires, it is a flame the size of a thumb; but when one with pure reason and the inner Spirit, it becomes in concentration as the point of a needle.

The soul can be thought as the part of a point of a hair which divided by a hundred were divided by a hundred again; and yet in this living soul there is the seed of Infinity.

The soul is not a man, nor a woman, nor what is neither a woman nor a man. When the soul takes the form of a body, by that same body the soul is bound.

The soul is born and unfolds in a body, with dreams and desires and the food of life. And then it is reborn in new bodies, in accordance with its former works.

The quality of the soul determines its future body: earthly or airy, heavy or light. Its thoughts and its actions can lead it to freedom, or lead it to bondage, in life after life.

But there is the God of forms infinite, and when a man knows God he is free from all bondage. He is the Creator of all, everliving in the mystery of his creation. He is beyond beginning and end, and in his glory all things are.

He is an incorporeal Spirit, but he can be seen by a heart which is pure. Being and non-being come from him and he is the Creator of all. He is God, the God of love, and when a man knows him then he leaves behind his bodies of transmigration.

PART 6

Some sages speak of the nature of things as the cause of the world, and others, in their delusion, speak of time. But it is by the glory of God that the Wheel of Brahman revolves in the universe.

The whole universe is ever in his power. He is pure consciousness, the creator of time: all-powerful, all-knowing. It is under his rule that the work of creation revolves in its evolution, and we have earth, and water, and ether, and fire and air.

God ended his work and he rested, and he made a bond of love between his soul and the soul of all things. And the ONE became one with the one, and the two, and the three and the eight, and with time and with the subtle mystery of the human soul.

His first works are bound by the three qualities, and he gives to each thing its place in nature. When the three are gone, the work is done, and then a greater work can begin.

His Being is the source of all being, the seed of all things that in this life have their life. He is beyond time and space, and yet he is the God of forms infinite who dwells in our inmost thoughts, and who is seen by those who love him.

He is beyond the tree of life and time, and things seen by mortal eyes; but the whole universe comes from him. He gives us truth and takes away evil, for he is the Lord of all good. Know that he is in the inmost of thy soul and that he is the home of thy immortality.

May we know the Lord of lords, the King of kings, the God of gods: God, the God of love, the Lord of all.

We cannot see how he works, or what are the tools of his work. Nothing can be compared with him, and how can anything be greater than he is? His power is shown in infinite ways, and how great is his work and wisdom!

No one was before he was, and no one has rule over him; because he is the source of all, and he is also the ruler of all.

May God who is hidden in nature, even as the silkworm is hidden in the web of silk he made, lead us to union with his own Spirit, with Brahman.

He is God, hidden in all beings, their inmost soul who is in all. He watches the works of creation, lives in all things, watches all things. He is pure consciousness, beyond the three conditions of nature, the ONE who rules the work of silence of many, the ONE who transforms one seed into many. Only those who see God in their soul attain the joy eternal.

He is the Eternal among things that pass away, pure Consciousness of conscious beings, the ONE who fulfils the prayers of many. By the vision of Sankhya and the harmony of Yoga a man knows God, and when a man knows God he is free from all fetters.

There the sun shines not, nor the moon, nor the stars; lightnings shine not there and much less earthly fire. From his light all these give light; and his radiance illumines all creation.

He is the wandering swan everlasting, the soul of all in the universe, the Spirit of fire in the ocean of life. To know him is to overcome death, and he is the only Path to life eternal.

He is the never-created Creator of all: he knows all. He is pure consciousness, the creator of time: all-powerful, all-knowing. He is the Lord of the soul and of nature and of the three conditions of nature. From him comes the transmigration of life and liberation: bondage in time and freedom in Eternity.

He is the God of light, immortal in his glory, pure consciousness, omnipresent, the loving protector of all. He is the everlasting ruler of the world: could there be any ruler but he?

Longing therefore for liberation, I go for refuge to God who by his grace reveals his own light; and who in the beginning created the god of creation and gave to him the sacred *Vedas*.

I go for refuge to God who is ONE in the silence of Eternity, pure radiance of beauty and perfection, in whom we find our peace. He is the bridge supreme which leads to immortality, and the Spirit of fire which burns the dross of lower life.

If ever for man it were possible to fold the tent of the sky, in that day he might be able to end his sorrow without the help of God.

By the power of inner harmony and by the grace of God Svetasvatara had the vision of Brahman. He then spoke to his nearest hermit-students about the supreme purification, about Brahman whom the seers adore.

This supreme mystery of the *Vedanta* which was revealed in olden times must only be given to one whose heart is pure and who is a pupil or a son.

If one has supreme love for God and also loves his master as God, then the light of this teaching shines in a great soul: it shines indeed in a great soul.

From the

MAITRI UPANISHAD

THIS is the knowledge of Brahman as found in all the *Upanishads* and as revealed by the sage Maitri.

The glorious Valakhilyas were pure and good, and once they asked Kratu Prajapati:

'Since this body is like a chariot without consciousness, who is the Spirit who has the power to make it conscious? Who is the driver of the chariot?'

Prajapati answered:

'There is a Spirit who is amongst the things of this world and yet he is above the things of this world. He is clear and pure, in the peace of a void of vastness. He is beyond the life of the body and the mind, never-born, never-dying, everlasting, ever ONE in his own greatness. He is the Spirit whose power gives consciousness to the body: he is the driver of the chariot.'

Then the Valakhilyas said:

'Master, how does this pure Being give consciousness to the unconscious body? How is he the driver of the chariot?'

Kratu Prajapati answered:

'Even as a man who is asleep awakes, but when he is asleep does not know that he is going to awake, so a part of the subtle invisible Spirit comes as a messenger to the body without the body being conscious of his arrival.

A part of Infinite Consciousness becomes our own finite consciousness with powers of discrimination and definition, and with false conceptions. He is in truth Prajapati and Visva, the Source of creation and the Universal in us all.

This Spirit is consciousness and gives consciousness to the body: he is the driver of the chariot.'   2. 3–5

The poets say that this is the Spirit who wanders on this earth from body to body, free from the light and darkness which follow our works. He is free because he is free from selfishness, and he is invisible, incomprehensible, hidden in darkness. He seems to work and not to be; but in truth he works not, and he is. He is in his own Being, pure, never-changing, never-moving, unpollutable; and in peace beyond desires he watches the drama of the universe. He is hidden behind the veil of the three conditions and constituents of the universe; but in the joy of his law of righteousness he is ever ONE, he is ever ONE.   2. 7

*

The Valakhilyas said:

'Master, you have spoken to us of the greatness of the Atman, the Spirit, the Supreme Soul; but what is the soul who is bound by the light or darkness which follow works, and who, born again from good and evil, rises or falls in its wanderings, under the impulse of two contrary powers?'

Prajapati answered:

'There is indeed the other soul composed of the elements of the body, the *bhutatman*, who is bound by the light or darkness which follow works and who, born again from good and evil, rises or falls in its wanderings under the impulse of two contrary powers.

And this is the explanation:

There are five subtle elements, *tan-matras*, and these are called elements. There are also five gross elements, *mahabhutas*, and these are also called elements. The union of these is called the human body. The human soul rules the body; but the immortal spiritual Soul is pure like a drop of water on a lotus leaf. The human soul is under the power of the three constituents and conditions of nature, and thus it falls into confusion. Because of this confusion the soul cannot become conscious of the God who dwells within and whose power gives us power to work. The soul is thus whirled along the rushing stream of muddy waters of the three conditions of nature, and becomes unsteady and wavering, filled with confusion and full of desires, lacking concentration and disturbed with pride. Whenever the soul has thoughts of "I" and "mine" it binds itself with its lower self, as a bird with the net of a snare.' 3. 2

*

'Brahman is', thus says the seer of Brahman.

'Brahman is the door', thus speaks the man of austere harmony whose sins have been washed away.

'OM is the glory of Brahman', says the man of contemplation for ever thinking on Brahman.

It is therefore by vision, by harmony, and by contemplation that Brahman is attained. 4. 4

*

In the beginning all was Brahman, ONE and infinite. He is beyond north and south, and east and west, and beyond what is above or below. His infinity is everywhere. In him there is neither above, nor across, nor below; and in him there is neither east nor west.

The Spirit supreme is immeasurable, inapprehensible, beyond conception, never-born, beyond reasoning, beyond thought. His vastness is the vastness of space.

At the end of the worlds, all things sleep: he alone is awake in Eternity. Then from his infinite space new worlds arise and awake, a universe which is a vastness of thought. In the consciousness of Brahman the universe is, and into him it returns.

He is seen in the radiance of the sun in the sky, in the brightness of fire on earth, and in the fire of life that burns the food of life. Therefore it has been said:

He who is in the sun, and in the fire and in the heart of man is ONE. He who knows this is one with the ONE. 6. 17

*

When a wise man has withdrawn his mind from all things without, and when his spirit of life has peacefully left inner sensations, let him rest in peace, free from the movements of will and desire. Since the living being called the spirit of life has come from that which is greater than the spirit of life, let the spirit of life surrender itself into what is called *turya*, the fourth condition of consciousness. For it has been said:

There is something beyond our mind which abides in silence within our mind. It is the supreme mystery beyond thought. Let one's mind and one's subtle body rest upon that and not rest on anything else. 6. 19

*

There are two ways of contemplation of Brahman: in sound and in silence. By sound we go to silence. The sound of Brahman is OM. With OM we go to the End: the silence of Brahman. The End is immortality, union and peace.

Even as a spider reaches the liberty of space by means of its own thread, the man of contemplation by means of OM reaches freedom. 6. 22

*

The sound of Brahman is OM. At the end of OM there is silence. It is a silence of joy. It is the end of the journey where fear and sorrow are no more: steady, motionless, never-falling, ever-lasting, immortal. It is called the omnipresent Vishnu.

In order to reach the Highest, consider in adoration the sound and the silence of Brahman. For it has been said:

God is sound and silence. His name is OM. Attain therefore contemplation – contemplation in silence on him. 6. 23

*

Even as fire without fuel finds peace in its resting-place, when thoughts become silence the soul finds peace in its own source.

And when a mind which longs for truth finds the peace of its own source, then those false inclinations cease which were the result of former actions done in the delusion of the senses.

Samsara, the transmigration of life, takes place in one's own mind. Let one therefore keep the mind pure, for what a man thinks that he becomes: this is a mystery of Eternity.

A quietness of mind overcomes good and evil works, and in quietness the soul is ONE: then one feels the joy of Eternity.

If men thought of God as much as they think of the world, who would not attain liberation?

The mind of man is of two kinds, pure and impure: impure when in the bondage of desire, pure when free from desire.

When the mind is silent, beyond weakness or non-concentration, then it can enter into a world which is far beyond the mind: the highest End.

The mind should be kept in the heart as long as it has not reached the Highest End. This is wisdom, and this is liberation. Everything else is only words.

Words cannot describe the joy of the soul whose impurities are cleansed in deep contemplation – who is one with his Atman, his own Spirit. Only those who feel this joy know what it is.

Even as water becomes one with water, fire with fire, and air with air, so the mind becomes one with the Infinite Mind and thus attains final freedom.

Mind is indeed the source of bondage and also the source of liberation. To be bound to things of this world: this is bondage. To be free from them : this is liberation.

from 6. 24

Glory be unto Agni, the god of fire, who dwells in the earth, who remembers the world. Give this world to him who adores thee.

Glory be unto Vayu, the god of the wind, who dwells in the air, who remembers this world. Give this world to him who adores thee.

Glory be unto Aditya, the god of the sun, who dwells in the sky, who remembers this world. Give this world to him who adores thee.

from 6. 35

From the
KAUSHITAKI UPANISHAD

WHEN a man is speaking, he cannot be breathing: this is the sacrifice of breath to speech. And when a man is breathing he cannot be speaking: this is the sacrifice of speech to breath.

These are the two never-ending immortal offerings of man, whether he is awake or whether he is asleep.   2. 5

These are the three adorations of the all-conquering Kaushitaki:

At the rising of the sun he said, 'You who give liberty, make me free from my sins'.

When the sun was mid-way in heaven he said, 'You who are on high and give liberty, set me on high and make me free from my sins'.

At the hour of sunset he uttered this prayer, 'You who give full liberty, make me fully free from my sins'.   2. 7

When the fire burns, Brahman shines; and when the fire dies, Brahman goes. Its light goes to the sun, and its breath of life to the wind.

When the sun shines, Brahman shines; and when the sun sets, Brahman goes. Its light goes to the moon, and its breath of life to the wind.

When the moon shines, Brahman shines; and when the moon sets, Brahman goes. Its light goes to a flash of lightning, and its breath of life to the wind.

When a flash of lightning shines, Brahman shines; and when it goes, Brahman goes. Its light goes to the regions of heaven, and its breath of life to the wind.   2. 12

*

Pratardana, the son of Devadasa, fought the inner fight with all his soul and thus he reached the house of Indra, the house of the love of God.

Indra said to him: 'Pratardana, ask for a gift.' To this Pratardana replied: 'I ask for that gift which you think is best for mankind.'

'A master imposes not a gift upon his pupil,' said Indra, 'ask for any gift you like.'

'I shall then not have a gift,' said Pratardana.

But Indra left not the path of truth, for God is truth. He thus said to Pratardana: 'Know me, for this is the best for man: to know God.'   3. 1

Then Indra spoke:

I am the breath of life, and I am the consciousness of life. Adore me and think of me as life and immortality.

The breath of life is one:

When we speak, life speaks.

When we see, life sees.

When we hear, life hears.

When we think, life thinks.

When we breathe, life breathes.

And there is something greater than the breath of life.

For one can live without speech: we can see the dumb.

One can live without sight: we can see the blind.

One can live without hearing: we can see the deaf.

One can live without a right mind: we can see those who are mad.

But it is the consciousness of life which becomes the breath of life and gives life to a body. The breath of life is the consciousness of life, and the consciousness of life is the breath of life.   3. 2–3

When consciousness rules speech, with speech we can speak all words.

When consciousness rules breath, with inbreath we can smell all perfumes.

When consciousness rules the eye, with the eye we can see all forms.

When consciousness rules the ear, with the ear we can hear all sounds.

When consciousness rules the tongue, with the tongue we can savour all tastes.

When consciousness rules the mind, with the mind we can think all thoughts.   3. 6

*

It is not speech which we should want to know: we should know the speaker.

It is not things seen which we should want to know: we should know the seer.

It is not sounds which we should want to know: we should know the hearer.

It is not mind which we should want to know: WE SHOULD KNOW THE THINKER.   3. 8

From the

TAITTIRIYA UPANISHAD

I will speak words of truth and the words of the divine law shall be on my lips.   I. I

Master and *disciple*.
May the light of sacred knowledge illumine us, and may we attain the glory of wisdom.   I. 3

O Lord, let me come unto thee and come thou unto me, O Lord. In thy waters, O my Lord, may I wash my sins away.
     I. 4

What is needful?
Righteousness, and sacred learning and teaching.
Truth, and sacred learning and teaching.
Meditation, and sacred learning and teaching.
Self-control, and sacred learning and teaching.
Peace, and sacred learning and teaching.
Ritual, and sacred learning and teaching.
Humanity, and sacred learning and teaching.

*

Satyavacas, the Truthful, says: 'Truth.'
Taponitya, the Austere, says: 'Austerity.'
But Naka, who is beyond pain, says: 'Learning and teaching. For they are austerity, for they are austerity.'   I. 9

*

He who knows Brahman who is Truth, consciousness, and

infinite joy, hidden in the inmost of our soul and in the highest heaven, enjoys all things he desires in communion with the all-knowing Brahman. From Atman – Brahman – in the beginning came space. From space came air. From air, fire. From fire, water. From water came solid earth. From earth came living plants. From plants food and seed; and from seed and food came a living being, man.   2. 1

Who denies God, denies himself. Who affirms God, affirms himself.   2. 6

Joy comes from God. Who could live and who could breathe if the joy of Brahman filled not the universe?   2.7

If a man places a gulf between himself and God, this gulf will bring fear. But if a man finds the support of the In-visible and Ineffable, he is free from fear.   2. 7

Words and mind go to him, but reach him not and re-turn. But he who knows the joy of Brahman, fears no more.   2. 9

*

Once Bhrigu Varuni went to his father Varuna and said: 'Father, explain to me the mystery of Brahman.'

Then his father spoke to him of the food of the earth, of the breath of life, of the one who sees, of the one who hears, of the mind that knows, and of the one who speaks. And he further said to him: 'Seek to know him from whom all beings have come, by whom they all live, and unto whom they all return. He is Brahman.'

So Bhrigu went and practised *tapas*, spiritual prayer. Then he thought that Brahman was the food of the earth: for from the earth all beings have come, by food of the earth they all live, and unto the earth they all return.

After this he went again to his father Varuna and said:

'Father, explain further to me the mystery of Brahman.' To him his father answered: 'Seek to know Brahman by *tapas*, by prayer, because Brahman is prayer.'

So Bhrigu went and practised *tapas*, spiritual prayer. Then he thought that Braham was life: for from life all beings have come, by life they all live, and unto life they all return.

After this he went again to his father Varuna and said: 'Father, explain further to me the mystery of Brahman.' To him his father answered: 'Seek to know Brahman by *tapas*, by prayer, because Brahman is prayer.'

So Bhrigu went and practised *tapas*, spiritual prayer. Then he thought that Brahman was mind: for from mind all beings have come, by mind they all live, and unto mind they all return.

After this he went again to his father Varuna and said: 'Father, explain further to me the mystery of Brahman.' To him his father answered: 'Seek to know Brahman by *tapas*, by prayer, because Brahman is prayer.'

So Bhrigu went and practised *tapas*, spiritual prayer. Then he thought that Brahman was reason: for from reason all beings have come, by reason they all live, and unto reason they all return.

He went again to his father, asked the same question, and received the same answer.

So Bhrigu went and practised *tapas*, spiritual prayer. And then he *saw* that Brahman is joy: for FROM JOY ALL BEINGS HAVE COME, BY JOY THEY ALL LIVE, AND UNTO JOY THEY ALL RETURN.

This was the vision of Bhrigu Varuni which came from the Highest; and he who sees this vision lives in the Highest.

3. 1–6

Oh, the wonder of joy!

I am the food of life, and I am he who eats the food of life: I am the two in ONE.

I am the first-born of the world of truth, born before the gods, born in the centre of immortality.

He who gives me is my salvation.

I am that food which eats the eater of food.

I have gone beyond the universe, and the light of the sun is my light. 3. 10. 6

From the

CHANDOGYA UPANISHAD

WHEREFROM do all these worlds come? They come from space. All beings arise from space, and into space they return: space is indeed their beginning, and space is their final end.   1. 9. 1

*

Prajapati, the Creator of all, rested in life-giving meditation over the worlds of his creation; and from them came the three *Vedas*. He rested in meditation and from those came the three sounds: BHUR, BHUVAS, SVAR, earth, air, and sky. He rested in meditation and from the three sounds came the sound OM. Even as all leaves come from a stem, all words come from the sound OM. OM is the whole universe. OM is in truth the whole universe.   2. 23. 2

*

Great is the Gayatri, the most sacred verse of the *Vedas*; but how much greater is the Infinity of Brahman! A quarter of his being is this whole vast universe: the other three quarters are his heaven of Immortality.   3. 12. 5

*

There is a Light that shines beyond all things on earth, beyond us all, beyond the heavens, beyond the highest, the very highest heavens. This is the Light that shines in our heart.   3. 13. 7

*

All this universe is in truth Brahman. He is the beginning and end and life of all. As such, in silence, give unto him adoration.

Man in truth is made of faith. As his faith is in this life, so he becomes in the beyond: with faith and vision let him work.

There is a Spirit that is mind and life, light and truth and vast spaces. He contains all works and desires and all perfumes and all tastes. He enfolds the whole universe, and in silence is loving to all.

This is the Spirit that is in my heart, smaller than a grain of rice, or a grain of barley, or a grain of mustard-seed, or a grain of canary-seed, or the kernel of a grain of canary-seed. This is the Spirit that is in my heart, greater than the earth, greater than the sky, greater than heaven itself, greater than all these worlds.

He contains all works and desires and all perfumes and all tastes. He enfolds the whole universe and in silence is loving to all. This is the Spirit that is in my heart, this is Brahman.

To him I shall come when I go beyond this life. And to him will come he who has faith and doubts not. Thus said Sandilya, thus said Sandilya.   3. 14

*

I go to the Imperishable Treasure: by his grace, by his grace, by his grace.

I go to the Spirit of life: by his grace, by his grace, by his grace.

I go to the Spirit of the earth: by his grace, by his grace, by his grace.

I go to the Spirit of the air: by his grace, by his grace, by his grace.

I go to the Spirit of the heavens: by his grace, by his grace, by his grace.   3. 15. 3

A man is a living sacrifice. The first twenty-four years of his life are the morning offering of the Soma-wine; because the holy Gayatri has twenty-four sounds, and the chanting of the Gayatri is heard in the morning offering. The Vasus, the gods of the earth, rule this offering. If a man should be ill during that time, he should pray: 'With the help of the Vasus, the powers of my life, may my morning offering last until my midday offering and may not my sacrifice perish whilst the Vasus are the powers of my life.'

The next forty-four years of his life are the midday offering of the Soma-wine; because the holy Trishtubh has forty-four sounds, and the chanting of the Trishtubh is heard with the midday offering. The Rudras, the gods of the air, rule this offering. If a man should be ill during that time, he should pray: 'With the help of the Rudras, the powers of my life, may my midday offering last until my evening offering, and may not my sacrifice perish whilst the Rudras are the powers of my life.'

The next forty-eight years of his life are the evening offering; because the holy Jagati has forty-eight sounds, and the chanting of the Jagati is heard with the evening offering. The Adityas, the gods of light, rule this offering. If a man should be ill during that time, he should pray: 'With the help of the Adityas, the powers of my life, let my evening offering last until the end of a long life; and may not my sacrifice perish whilst the Adityas are the powers of my life.'

Mahidasa Aitareya knew this when he used to say: 'Why should I suffer an illness when I am not going to die?' And he lived one hundred and sixteen years.   3. 16

*

We should consider that in the inner world Brahman is consciousness; and we should consider that in the outer world Brahman is space. These are the two meditations.

3. 18. 1

Once Satyakama went to his mother and said: 'Mother, I wish to enter upon the life of a religious student. Of what family am I?'

To him she answered: 'I do not know, my child, of what family thou art. In my youth, I was poor and served as a maid many masters, and then I had thee: I therefore do not know of what family thou art. My name is Jabala and thy name is Satyakama. Thou mayest call thyself Satyakama Jabala.'

The boy went to the Master Haridrumata Gautama and said: 'I want to become a student of sacred wisdom. May I come to you, Master?'

To him the Master asked: 'Of what family art thou, my son?'

'I do not know of what family I am,' answered Satyakama. 'I asked my mother and she said: "I do not know, my child, of what family thou art. In my youth, I was poor and served as a maid many masters, and then I had thee: I therefore do not know of what family thou art. My name is Jabala and thy name is Satyakama." I am therefore Satyakama Jabala, Master.'

To him Master Gautama said: 'Thou art a Brahman, since thou hast not gone away from truth. Come, my son, I will take thee as a student.'   4. 4

*

OM. There lived once a boy, Svetaketu Aruneya by name. One day his father spoke to him in this way: 'Svetaketu, go and become a student of sacred wisdom. There is no one in our family who has not studied the holy *Vedas* and who might only be given the name of Brahman by courtesy.'

The boy left at the age of twelve and, having learnt the *Vedas*, he returned home at the age of twenty-four, very proud of his learning and having a great opinion of himself.

His father, observing this, said to him: 'Svetaketu, my boy, you seem to have a great opinion of yourself, you think you are learned, and you are proud. Have you asked for that knowledge whereby what is not heard is heard, what is not thought is thought, and what is not known is known?'

'What is that knowledge, father?' asked Svetaketu.

'Just as by knowing a lump of clay, my son, all that is clay can be known, since any differences are only words and the reality is clay;

Just as by knowing a piece of gold all that is gold can be known, since any differences are only words and the reality is only gold;

And just as by knowing a piece of iron all that is iron is known, since any differences are only words and the reality is only iron.'

Svetaketu said: 'Certainly my honoured masters knew not this themselves. If they had known, why would they not have told me? Explain this to me, father.'

'So be it, my child.' 6. 1

*

'Bring me a fruit from this banyan tree.'

'Here it is, father.'

'Break it.'

'It is broken, Sir.'

'What do you see in it?'

'Very small seeds, Sir.'

'Break one of them, my son.'

'It is broken, Sir.'

'What do you see in it?'

'Nothing at all, Sir.'

Then his father spoke to him: 'My son, from the very essence in the seed which you cannot see comes in truth this vast banyan tree.

Believe me, my son, an invisible and subtle essence is the Spirit of the whole universe. That is Reality. That is Atman. THOU ART THAT.'

'Explain more to me, father,' said Svetaketu.

'So be it, my son.

Place this salt in water and come to me tomorrow morning.'

Svetaketu did as he was commanded, and in the morning his father said to him: 'Bring me the salt you put into the water last night.'

Svetaketu looked into the water, but could not find it, for it had dissolved.

His father then said: 'Taste the water from this side. How is it?'

'It is salt.'

'Taste it from the middle. How is it?'

'It is salt.'

'Taste it from that side. How is it?'

'It is salt.'

'Look for the salt again and come again to me.'

The son did so, saying: 'I cannot see the salt. I only see water.'

His father then said: 'In the same way, O my son, you cannot see the Spirit. But in truth he is here.

An invisible and subtle essence is the Spirit of the whole universe. That is Reality. That is Truth. THOU ART THAT.'

'Explain more to me, father.'

'So be it, my son.

Even as a man, O my son, who had been led blindfolded from his land of the Gandharas and then left in a desert place, might wander to the East and North and South, because he had been taken blindfolded and left in an unknown place, but if a good man took off his bandage and told him "In that direction is the land of the Gandharas, go in that direction," then, if he were a wise man, he would go asking from village to village until he would have reached his land of the Gandharas; so it happens in this world to a man who has a Master to direct him to the land of the Spirit. Such a man can say: "I shall wander in this world until I attain liberation; but then I shall go and reach my Home."

This invisible and subtle essence is the Spirit of the whole universe. That is Reality. That is Truth. THOU ART THAT.'

6. 12–14

Is there anything higher than thought?

Meditation is in truth higher than thought. The earth seems to rest in silent meditation; and the waters and the mountains and the sky and the heavens seem all to be in meditation. Whenever a man attains greatness on this earth, he has his reward according to his meditation.   7.6

*

When a man speaks words of truth he speaks words of greatness: know the nature of truth.

When a man knows, he can speak truth. He who does not know cannot speak truth: know the nature of knowledge.

When a man thinks then he can know. He who does not think does not know: know the nature of thought.

When a man has faith then he thinks. He who has not faith does not think: know the nature of faith.

Where there is progress one sees and has faith. Where there is no progress there is no faith: know the nature of progress.

Where there is creation there is progress. Where there is no creation there is no progress: know the nature of creation.

Where there is joy there is creation. Where there is no joy there is no creation: know the nature of joy.

Where there is the Infinite there is joy. There is no joy in the finite. Only in the Infinite there is joy: know the nature of the Infinite.

Where nothing else is seen, or heard, or known there is the Infinite. Where something else is seen, or heard, or known there is the finite. The Infinite is immortal; but the finite is mortal.

'Where does the Infinite rest?' On his own greatness, or not even on his own greatness.

In this world they call greatness the possession of cattle and horses, elephants and gold, servants and wives, lands and houses. But I do not call this greatness, for here one thing depends upon another.

But the Infinite is above and below, North and South and East and West. The Infinite is the whole universe.

I am above and below, North and South and East and West. I am the whole universe.

Atman is above and below, North and South and East and West. Atman is the whole universe.

He who sees, knows, and understands this, who finds in Atman, the Spirit, his love and his pleasure and his union and his joy, becomes a Master of himself. His freedom then is infinite.

But those who see not this become the servants of other masters and in the worlds that pass away attain not their liberation.   7. 16–25

*

OM. In the centre of the castle of Brahman, our own body, there is a small shrine in the form of a lotus-flower, and within can be found a small space. We should find who dwells there, and we should want to know him.

And if anyone asks, 'Who is he who dwells in a small shrine in the form of a lotus-flower in the centre of the castle of Brahman? Whom should we want to find and to know?' we can answer:

'The little space within the heart is as great as this vast universe. The heavens and the earth are there, and the sun, and the moon, and the stars; fire and lightning and winds are there; and all that now is and all that is not: for the whole universe is in Him and He dwells within our heart.'

And if they should say, 'If all things are in the castle of Brahman, all beings and all desires, what remains when old age overcomes the castle or when the life of the body is gone?' we can answer:

'The Spirit who is in the body does not grow old and does not die, and no one can ever kill the Spirit who is ever-lasting. This is the real castle of Brahman wherein dwells all the love of the universe. It is Atman, pure Spirit, beyond sorrow, old age, and death; beyond evil and hunger and thirst. It is Atman whose love is Truth, whose thoughts are Truth.

Even as here on earth the attendants of a king obey their king, and are with him wherever he is and go with him wherever he goes, so all love which is Truth and all thoughts of Truth obey the Atman, the Spirit. And even as here on earth all work done in time ends in time, so in the worlds to come even the good works of the past pass away. Therefore those who leave this world and have not found their soul, and that love which is Truth, find not their freedom in other worlds. But those who leave this world and have found their soul and that love which is Truth, for them there is the liberty of the Spirit, in this world and in the worlds to come.'

8. 1

*

There is a bridge between time and Eternity; and this bridge is Atman, the Spirit of man. Neither day nor night cross that bridge, nor old age, nor death nor sorrow.

Evil or sin cannot cross that bridge, because the world of the Spirit is pure. This is why when this bridge has been crossed, the eyes of the blind can see, the wounds of the wounded are healed, and the sick man becomes whole from his sickness.

To one who goes over that bridge, the night becomes like unto day; because in the worlds of the Spirit there is a Light which is everlasting.   8. 4. 1

*

'There is a Spirit which is pure and which is beyond old age and death; and beyond hunger and thirst and sorrow. This is Atman, the Spirit in man. All the desires of this Spirit are Truth. It is this Spirit that we must find and know: man must find his own Soul. He who has found and knows his Soul has found all the worlds, has achieved all his desires.' Thus spoke Prajapati.

The gods and the devils heard these words and they said: 'Come, let us go and find the Atman, let us find the Soul, so that we may obtain all our desires.'

Then Indra amongst the gods and Virochana amongst the devils went without telling each other to see Prajapati, carrying fuel in their hands as a sign that they wanted to be his pupils.

And so for thirty-two years they both lived with Prajapati the life of religious students. At the end of that time Prajapati asked them: 'Why have you been living the life of religious students?'

Indra and Virochana answered: 'People say that you know the Atman, a Spirit which is pure and which is beyond old age and death, and beyond hunger and thirst and sorrow, a Spirit whose desires are Truth and whose thoughts are Truth; and that you say that this Spirit must be found and known, because when he is found all the worlds are found and all desires are obtained. This is why we have been living here as your pupils.'

Prajapati said to them: 'What you see when you look into another person's eyes, that is the Atman, immortal, beyond fear, that is Brahman.'

'And who is he whom we see when we look in water or in a mirror?' they asked.

'The same is seen in all,' he answered. And then he said to them: 'Go and look at yourselves in a bowl of water and ask me anything you want to know about the Atman, your own self.'

The two went and looked in a bowl of water. 'What do you see?' asked Prajapati.

'We see ourselves clearly from our hair down to our nails,' they said.

'Adorn yourselves and dress in clothes of beauty,' said Prajapati, 'and look at yourselves again in a bowl of water.'

They did so and looked again in the bowl of water. 'What do you see?' asked Prajapati.

'We see ourselves as we are,' they answered, 'adorned and dressed in clothes of beauty.'

'This is the Immortal beyond all fear: this is Brahman,' said Prajapati.

Then they left with peace in their hearts.

Prajapati looked at them and said: 'They have seen but they have not understood. They have not found the Atman, their soul. Anyone who holds their belief, be he god or devil, shall perish.'

Then Virochana went to the devils full of self-satisfaction, and gave them this teaching: 'We ourselves are our own bodies, and those must be made happy on earth. It is our bodies that should be in glory, and it is for them that we should have servants. He who makes his body happy, he who for his body has servants, he is well in this world and also in the world to come.'

That is why when here on earth a man will not give any gifts, when a man has no faith and will not sacrifice, people say 'This man is a devil'; for this is in truth their devilish doctrine. They dress their dead bodies with fine garments, and glorify them with perfumes and ornaments, thinking that thereby they will conquer the other world.

But before Indra had returned to the gods he saw the danger of this teaching and he thought: 'If our self, our Atman, is the body, and is dressed in clothes of beauty when the body is, and is covered with ornaments when the body is, then when the body is blind the self is blind, and when the body is lame the self is lame; and when the body dies, our self dies. I cannot find any joy in this doctrine.'

He therefore went back to Prajapati with fuel in hand as a sign that he wanted to be his pupil.

'Why have you returned, great Maghavan?' asked Prajapati. 'You went away with Virochana with peace in your heart.'

Indra replied: 'Even as the Atman, the self, our soul, is dressed in clothes of beauty when the body is, and is covered with ornaments when the body is, when the body is blind the self is blind, and when the body is lame the self is lame, and when the body dies the self dies. I cannot find any joy in this doctrine.'

'It is even so, Maghavan,' said Prajapati. 'I will teach you a higher doctrine. Live with me for another thirty-two years.'

Indra was with Prajapati for another thirty-two years, and then Prajapati said: 'The spirit that wanders in joy in the land of dreams, that is the Atman, that is the Immortal beyond fear: that is Brahman.'

Then Indra left with peace in his heart; but before he had returned to the gods he saw the danger of this teaching and he thought: 'Even if in dreams when the body is blind the self is not blind, or when the body is lame the self is not lame, and does not indeed suffer the limitations of the body, so that when the body is killed the self is not killed; yet in dreams the self may seem to be killed and to suffer, and to feel much pain and weep. I cannot find any joy in this doctrine.'

He therefore went with fuel in hand back to Prajapati, who said to him: 'You left, Maghavan, with peace in your heart; why have you returned?'

Indra replied: 'Even if in dreams when the body is blind the Atman is not blind, or when the body is lame the Atman is not lame, and indeed does not suffer the limitations of the body, so that when the body is killed the self is not killed; yet in dreams the self may seem to be killed and suffer, and to feel much pain and weep. I cannot find any joy in this doctrine.'

'What you say is true, Maghavan,' said Prajapati. 'I will teach you a higher doctrine. Live with me for another thirty-two years.'

Indra was with Prajapati another thirty-two years.

And then Prajapati said:

'The spirit who is sleeping without dreams in the silent quietness of deep sleep, that is the Atman, that is the Immortal beyond fear: that is Brahman.'

Then Indra left with peace in his heart, but before he had reached the gods he saw the danger of this teaching and he thought: 'If a man is in deep sleep without dreams he cannot even say "I am" and he cannot know anything. He in truth falls into nothingness. I cannot find any joy in this doctrine.' And he went again to Prajapati with fuel in hand.

'Why have you returned, Maghavan? You left with peace in your heart,' asked Prajapati.

Indra replied: 'If a man is in deep sleep without dreams he cannot even say "I am" and he cannot know anything. He in truth falls into nothingness. I cannot find any joy in this doctrine.'

'What you say is true, Maghavan,' said Prajapati. 'I will teach you a higher doctrine, the highest that can be taught. Live with me now for five years.'

And Indra lived with Prajapati for five years. He lived with Prajapati a total of years one hundred and one. This is why people say: 'Great Indra lived with Prajapati the life of chastity of a Brahmacharya spiritual student for one hundred and one years.'

Prajapati then spoke to Indra:

'It is true that the body is mortal, that it is under the power of death; but it is also the dwelling of Atman, the Spirit of immortal life. The body, the house of the Spirit, is under the power of pleasure and pain; and if a man is ruled by his body then this man can never be free. But when a man is in the joy of the Spirit, in the Spirit which is ever free, then this man is free from all bondage, the bondage of pleasure and pain.

The wind has not a body, nor lightning, nor thunder, nor clouds; but when those rise into the higher spheres then they find their body of light. In the same way, when the soul is in silent quietness it arises and leaves the body, and reaching the Spirit Supreme finds there its body of light. It is the land of infinite liberty where, beyond its mortal body, the Spirit of man is free. There can he laugh and sing of his glory with ethereal women and friends. He enjoys ethereal chariots and forgets the cart of his body on earth. For as a beast is attached to a cart, so on earth the soul is attached to a body.

Know that when the eye looks into space it is the Spirit of man that sees: the eye is only the organ of sight. When one says "I feel this perfume," it is the Spirit that feels: he uses the organ of smell. When one says "I am speaking," it is the Spirit that speaks: the voice is the organ of speech. When one says "I am hearing," it is the Spirit that hears: the ear is the organ of hearing. And when one says "I think," it is the Spirit that thinks: the mind is the organ of thought. It is because of the light of the Spirit that the human mind can see, and can think, and enjoy this world.

All the gods in the heaven of Brahman adore in contemplation their Infinite Spirit Supreme. This is why they have all joy, and all the worlds and all desires. And the man who on this earth finds and knows Atman, his own Self, has all his holy desires and all the worlds and all joy.'

Thus spoke Prajapati. Thus in truth spoke Prajapati.

8. 7–12

From the

BRIHAD-ARANYAKA UPANISHAD

longest of upanishads (handwritten)

> From delusion lead me to Truth.
> From darkness lead me to Light.
> From death lead me to immortality.   I. 3. 28

THIS universe is a trinity and this is made of name, form, and action.

The source of all names is the word, for it is by the word that all names are spoken. The word is behind all names, even as Brahman is behind the word.

The source of all forms is the eye, for it is by the eye that all forms are seen. The eye is behind all forms, even as Brahman is behind the eye.

The source of all actions is the body, for it is by the body that all actions are done. The body is behind all actions, even as Brahman is behind the body.

Those three are one, ATMAN, the Spirit of life; and ATMAN, although one, is those three.

The Immortal is veiled by the real. The Spirit of life is the immortal. Name and form are the real, and by them the Spirit is veiled.   I. 6

*

Once Gargya, a Brahmin proud of his learning, went to Ajatasatru, the king of Benares and said: I am willing to teach you about Brahman.

I will give you a thousand gifts, if you can, said the king, and then the people will run and say: 'Our king's bounty is as great as that of king Janaka.'

So Gargya began and said: There is a spirit in the sun high above, and that spirit I adore as Brahman.

How can you say that? replied Ajatasatru. I only consider

127

Deals w/basic indiv. self & universal self (handwritten)
3 stages of spiritual life (handwritten)
learning, teaching, meditation (handwritten)

the sun as the ruler of radiance, the source of all beings on earth.

Then Gargya said: There is a spirit in the moon far away, and that spirit I adore as Brahman.

Ajatasatru answered: I only consider the moon as the ruler of the sacred Soma-wine dressed in whiteness.

There is a spirit in lightning, then said Gargya, and that spirit I adore as Brahman.

I only consider lightning, said Ajatasatru, as a thing of brightness.

Gargya said: There is a spirit in the ethereal spaces, and that spirit I adore as Brahman.

How can you say that? replied Ajatasatru. I only consider the ethereal space as a non-evolving fulness.

Gargya said: There is a spirit in the wind, and that spirit I adore as Brahman.

Ajatasatru answered: I only consider the winds as the unconquerable army of powerful Indra.

Gargya said: There is a spirit in fire, and that spirit I adore as Brahman.

I only consider fire, said Ajatasatru, as a great power.

Gargya said: There is a spirit in water, and that spirit I adore as Brahman.

Ajatasatru answered: I only consider water as a beautiful reflection.

Gargya said: There is a spirit in a mirror, and that spirit I adore as Brahman.

I only consider a mirror, said Ajatasatru, as something brilliant.

Gargya said: There is a spirit in the sound of the steps of man, and that spirit I adore as Brahman.

How can you say that? said Ajatasatru. I only consider that sound as a sign of life.

Gargya said: There is a spirit in the quarters of heaven, and that spirit I adore as Brahman.

I only consider the quarters of heaven, said Ajatasatru, as friends who are ever with us.

There is a spirit which is a shadow, said Gargya, and that spirit I adore as Brahman.

How can you say that? said Ajatasatru. I only consider this shadow as death.

Gargya said: There is a spirit in the human body, and that spirit I adore as Brahman.

I only consider a body, said Ajatasatru, as the covering of a soul.

Is this all? asked Ajatasatru.

Gargya replied: This is all.

If this is all, we know nothing, said Ajatasatru.

On hearing this, Gargya said: Allow me to be your pupil.

It is indeed contrary to custom, said Ajatasatru, that a Brahmin should go to a Kshatriya for instruction. But come, I will in truth teach you about Brahman.

And he arose and took him by the hand, and the two walking together came up to a man who was in deep sleep. They called him by different names such as 'You great man dressed in whiteness, you Soma the king', but he did not rise. Then Ajatasatru shook him with his hand and he awoke.

When this man was asleep, said Ajatasatru, where had his consciousness gone; and when he awoke, wherefrom did it return? But Gargya did not know.

Then spoke Ajatasatru:

When a man is asleep his soul takes the consciousness of the several senses and goes to rest with them on the Supreme Spirit who is in the human heart. When all the senses are quiet the man is said to be asleep. Then the soul holds the powers of life – breath, voice, eye, ear, and mind – and they rest in quietness.

When the soul is in the land of dreams, then all the worlds belong to the soul. A man can be a great king or a great Brahmin, and live in conditions high or low. And even as a great king of this earth takes his attendants with him and goes about his dominions wherever he desires, so the soul of man takes the powers of life with him and wanders in the land of dreams according to his desires.

When a man is in deep sleep and all consciousness is gone through the seventy-two thousand little channels which lead to the centre of the heart from its circumference, then the soul rests in the covering around the heart. And as a prince, or a king, or a great Brahmin might find the peace of a fulness of joy, so the soul of man has now found peace.

Even as airy threads come from a spider, or small sparks come from a fire, so from Atman, the Spirit in man, come all the powers of life, all the worlds, all the gods: all beings. To know the Atman is to know the mystery of the *Upanishads*: the Truth of truth. The powers of life are truth and their Truth is Atman, the Spirit.   2. 1. 1–20

*

'Maitreyi,' said one day Yajñavalkya to his wife, 'I am going to leave this present life, and retire to a life of meditation. Let me settle my possessions upon you and Katyayani.'

'If all the earth filled with riches belonged to me, O my Lord,' said Maitreyi, 'should I thereby attain life eternal?'

'Certainly not,' said Yajñavalkya, 'your life would only be as is the life of wealthy people. In wealth there is no hope of life eternal.'

Maitreyi said: 'What should I then do with possessions that cannot give me life eternal? Give me instead your knowledge, o my Lord.'

On hearing this Yajñavalkya exclaimed: 'Dear you are to me, beloved, and dear are the words you say. Come, sit down and I will teach; but hear my words with deep attention.'

Then spoke Yajñavalkya:

'In truth, it is not for the love of a husband that a husband is dear; but for the love of the Soul in the husband that a husband is dear.

It is not for the love of a wife that a wife is dear; but for the love of the Soul in the wife that a wife is dear.

It is not for the love of children that children are dear; but for the love of the Soul in children that children are dear.

It is not for the love of riches that riches are dear; but for the love of the Soul in riches that riches are dear.

It is not for the love of religion that religion is dear; but for the love of the Soul in religion that religion is dear.

It is not for the love of power that power is dear; but for the love of the Soul in power that power is dear.

It is not for the love of the heavens that the heavens are dear; but for the love of the Soul in the heavens that the heavens are dear.

It is not for the love of the gods that the gods are dear; but for the love of the Soul in the gods that the gods are dear.

It is not for the love of creatures that creatures are dear; but for the love of the Soul in creatures that creatures are dear.

It is not for the love of the all that the all is dear; but for the love of the Soul in the all that the all is dear.

It is the Soul, the Spirit, the Self, that must be seen and be heard and have our thoughts and meditation, O Maitreyi. When the Soul is seen and heard, is thought upon and is known, then all that is becomes known.

Religion will abandon the man who thinks that religion is apart from the Soul.

Power will abandon the man who thinks that power is apart from the Soul.

The gods will abandon the man who thinks that the gods are apart from the Soul.

Creatures will abandon the man who thinks that creatures are apart from the Soul.

And all will abandon the man who thinks that the all is apart from the Soul.

Because religion, power, heavens, beings, gods and all rest on the Soul.

As when a drum is being beaten its sounds cannot be

holden, but by seizing the drum or the beater of the drum the sounds are holden;

As when a conch is being blown its sounds cannot be holden, but by seizing the conch or the blower of the conch the sounds are holden;

As when a lute is being played its sounds cannot be holden, but by seizing the lute or the player of the lute the sounds are holden;

So it is with the Spirit, the Soul.

As when a lump of salt is thrown into water and therein being dissolved it cannot be grasped again, but wherever the water is taken it is found salt, in the same way, O Maitreyi, the supreme Spirit is an ocean of pure consciousness boundless and infinite. Arising out of the elements, into them it returns again: there is no consciousness after death.'

Thus spoke Yajñavalkya.

Thereupon Maitreyi said: 'I am amazed, O my Lord, to hear that after death there is no consciousness.'

To this Yajñavalkya replied: 'I am not speaking words of amazement; but sufficient for wisdom is what I say.

For where there seems to be a duality, there one sees another, one hears another, one feels another's perfume, one thinks of another, one knows another. But when all has become Spirit, one's own Self, how and whom could one see? How and whom could one hear? How and of whom could one feel the perfume? How and to whom could one speak? How and whom could one know? How can one know him who knows all? How can the Knower be known?'   2. 4

THE SUPREME TEACHING

PROLOGUE

To Janaka king of Videha came once Yajñavalkya meaning
to keep in silence the supreme secret wisdom. But once,
when Janaka and Yajñavalkya had been holding a discussion
at the offering of the sacred fire, Yajñavalkya promised to
grant the king any wish and the king chose to ask questions
according to his desire. Therefore Janaka, king of Videha, began and asked this question:

Yajñavalkya, what is the light of man?

The sun is his light, O king, he answered. It is by the
light of the sun that a man rests, goes forth, does his work,
and returns.

This is so in truth, Yajñavalkya. And when the sun is set,
what is then the light of man?

The moon then becomes his light, he replied. It is by
the light of the moon that a man rests, goes forth, does his
work, and returns.

This is so in truth, Yajñavalkya. And when the sun and
the moon are set, what is then the light of man?

Fire then becomes his light. It is by the light of fire that
a man rests, goes forth, does his work, and returns.

And when the sun and the moon are set, Yajñavalkya,
and the fire has sunk down, what is then the light of man?

Voice then becomes his light; and by the voice as his
light he rests, goes forth, does his work and returns. Therefore in truth, O king, when a man cannot see even his own
hand, if he hears a voice after that he wends his way.

This is so in truth, Yajñavalkya. And when the sun is set,
Yajñavalkya, and the moon is also set, and the fire has
sunk down, and the voice is silent, what is then the light of
man?

The Soul then becomes his light; and by the light of the Soul he rests, goes forth, does his work, and returns.

What is the Soul? asked then the king of Videha.

WAKING AND DREAMING

Yajñavalkya spoke:

It is the consciousness of life. It is the light of the heart. For ever remaining the same, the Spirit of man wanders in the world of waking life and also in the world of dreams. He seems to wander in thought. He seems to wander in joy.

But in the rest of deep sleep he goes beyond this world and beyond its fleeting forms.

For in truth when the Spirit of man comes to life and takes a body, then he is joined with mortal evils; but when at death he goes beyond, then he leaves evil behind.

The Spirit of man has two dwellings: this world and the world beyond. There is also a third dwelling-place: the land of sleep and dreams. Resting in this borderland the Spirit of man can behold his dwelling in this world and in the other world afar, and wandering in this borderland he beholds behind him the sorrows of this world and in front of him he sees the joys of the beyond.

DREAMS

When the Spirit of man retires to rest, he takes with him materials from this all-containing world, and he creates and destroys in his own glory and radiance. Then the Spirit of man shines in his own light.

In that land there are no chariots, no teams of horses, nor roads; but he creates his own chariots, his teams of horses, and roads. There are no joys in that region, and no pleasures nor delights; but he creates his own joys, his own pleasures and delights. In that land there are no lakes, no lotus-ponds, nor streams; but he creates his own lakes, his lotus-ponds, and streams. For the Spirit of man is Creator.

It was said in these verses:

Abandoning his body by the gate of dreams, the Spirit beholds in awaking his senses sleeping. Then he takes his own light and returns to his home, this Spirit of golden radiance, the wandering swan everlasting.

Leaving his nest below in charge of the breath of life, the immortal Spirit soars afar from his nest. He moves in all regions wherever he loves, this Spirit of golden radiance, the wandering swan everlasting.

And in the region of dreams, wandering above and below, the Spirit makes for himself innumerable subtle creations. Sometimes he seems to rejoice in the love of fairy beauties, sometimes he laughs or beholds awe-inspiring terrible visions.

People see his field of pleasure; but he can never be seen.

So they say that one should not wake up a person suddenly, for hard to heal would he be if the Spirit did not return. They say also that dreams are like the waking state, for what is seen when awake is seen again in a dream. What is true is that the Spirit shines in his own light.

'I give you a thousand gifts,' said then the king of Videha, 'but tell me of the higher wisdom that leads to liberation.'

When the Spirit of man has had his joy in the land of dreams, and in his wanderings there has beholden good and evil, he then returns to this world of waking. But whatever he has seen does not return with him, for the Spirit of man is free.

And when he has had his joy in this world of waking and in his wanderings here has beholden good and evil, he returns by the same path again to the land of dreams.

Even as a great fish swims along the two banks of a river, first along the eastern bank and then the western bank, in the same way the Spirit of man moves along beside his two dwellings: this waking world and the land of sleep and dreams.

DEEP SLEEP

Even as a falcon or an eagle, after soaring in the sky, folds his wings for he is weary, and flies down to his nest, even so the Spirit of man hastens to that place of rest where the soul has no desires and the Spirit sees no dreams.

What was seen in a dream, all the fears of waking, such as being slain or oppressed, pursued by an elephant or falling into an abyss, is seen to be a delusion. But when like a king or a god the Spirit feels 'I am all,' then he is in the highest world. It is the world of the Spirit, where there are no desires, all evil has vanished, and there is no fear.

As a man in the arms of the woman beloved feels only peace all around, even so the Soul in the embrace of Atman, the Spirit of vision, feels only peace all around. All desires are attained, since the Spirit that is all has been attained, no desires are there, and there is no sorrow.

There a father is a father no more, nor is a mother there a mother; the worlds are no longer worlds, nor the gods are gods any longer. There the *Vedas* disappear; and a thief is not a thief, nor is a slayer a slayer; the outcast is not an outcast, nor the base-born a base-born; the pilgrim is not a pilgrim and the hermit is not a hermit; because the Spirit of man has crossed the lands of good and evil, and has passed beyond the sorrows of the heart.

There the Spirit sees not, but though seeing not he sees. How could the Spirit not see if he is the All? But there is no duality there, nothing apart for him to see.

There the Spirit feels no perfumes, yet feeling no perfumes he feels them. How could the Spirit feel no perfumes if he is the All? But there is no duality there, no perfumes, apart for him to feel.

There the Spirit tastes not, yet tasting not he tastes. How could the Spirit not taste if he is the All? But there is no duality there, nothing apart for him to taste.

There the Spirit speaks not, yet speaking not he speaks. How could the Spirit not speak if he is the All? But there is no duality there, nothing apart for him to speak to.

There the Spirit hears not, yet hearing not he hears. How could the Spirit not hear if he is the All? But there is no duality there, nothing apart for him to hear.

There the Spirit thinks not, yet thinking not he thinks.

How could the Spirit not think if he is the All? But there is no duality there, nothing apart for him to think.

There the Spirit touches not, yet touching not he touches. How could the Spirit not touch if he is the All? But there is no duality there, nothing apart for him to touch.

There the Spirit knows not, yet knowing not he knows. How could the Spirit not know if he is the All? But there is no duality there, nothing apart for him to know.

For only where there seems to be a duality, there one sees another, one feels another's perfume, one tastes another, one speaks to another, one listens to another, one touches another and one knows another.

But in the ocean of Spirit the seer is alone beholding his own immensity.

This is the world of Brahman, O king. This is the path supreme. This is the supreme treasure. This is the world supreme. This is the supreme joy. On a portion of that joy all other beings live.

He who in this world attains success and wealth, who is Lord of men and enjoys all human pleasures, has reached the supreme human joy.

But a hundred times greater than the human joy is the joy of those who have attained the heaven of the ancestors.

A hundred times greater than the joy of the heaven of the ancestors is the joy of the heaven of the celestial beings.

A hundred times greater than the joy of the heaven of the celestial beings is the joy of the gods who have attained divinity through holy works.

A hundred times greater than the joy of the gods who have attained divinity through holy works is the joy of the gods who were born divine, and of him who has sacred wisdom, who is pure and free from desire.

A hundred times greater than the joy of the gods who were born divine is the joy of the world of the Lord of Creation, and of him who has sacred wisdom, who is pure and free from desire.

And a hundred times greater than the joy of the Lord of Creation is the joy of the world of Brahman, and of him who has sacred wisdom, who is pure and free from desire.

This is the joy supreme, this is the world of the Spirit, O king.

'I give you a thousand gifts,' said then the king of Videha: 'but tell me of the higher wisdom that leads to liberation.'

And Yajñavalkya was afraid and thought: Intelligent is the king. He has cut me off from all retreat.

When the Spirit of man has had his joy in the land of dreams, and in his wanderings there has beholden good and evil, he returns once again to this the world of waking.

DEATH

Even as a heavy-laden cart moves on groaning, even so the cart of the human body, wherein lives the Spirit, moves on groaning when a man is giving up the breath of life.

When the body falls into weakness on account of old age or disease, even as a mango-fruit, or the fruit of the holy fig-tree, is loosened from its stem, so the Spirit of man is loosened from the human body and returns by the same way to Life, wherefrom he came.

As when a king is coming, the nobles and officers, the charioteers and heads of the village prepare for him food and drink and royal lodgings, saying 'The king is coming, the king is approaching,' in the same way all the powers of life wait for him who knows this and say: 'The Spirit is coming, the Spirit is approaching.'

And as when a king is going to depart, the nobles and officers, the charioteers and the heads of the village assemble around him, even so all the powers of life gather about the soul when a man is giving up the breath of life.

When the human soul falls into weakness and into seeming unconsciousness all the powers of life assemble around. The soul gathers these elements of life-fire and enters into the heart. And when the Spirit that lives in the eye has returned to his own source, then the soul knows no more forms.

Then a person's powers of life become one and people say: 'he sees no more.' His powers of life become one and people say: 'he feels perfumes no more.' His powers of life become one and people say: 'he tastes no more.' His powers of life become one and people say: 'he speaks no more.' His powers of life become one and people say: 'he hears no more.' His powers of life become one and people say: 'he thinks no more.' His powers of life become one and people say: 'he touches no more.' His powers of life become one and people say: 'he knows no more.'

Then at the point of the heart a light shines, and this light illumines the soul on its way afar. When departing, by the head, or by the eye or other parts of the body, life arises and follows the soul, and the powers of life follow life. The soul becomes conscious and enters into Consciousness. His wisdom and works take him by the hand, and the knowledge known of old.

Even as a caterpillar, when coming to the end of a blade of grass, reaches out to another blade of grass and draws itself over to it, in the same way the Soul, leaving the body and unwisdom behind, reaches out to another body and draws itself over to it.

And even as a worker in gold, taking an old ornament, moulds it into a form newer and fairer, even so the Soul, leaving the body and unwisdom behind, goes into a form newer and fairer: a form like that of the ancestors in heaven, or of the celestial beings, or of the gods of light, or of the Lord of Creation, or of Brahma the Creator supreme, or a form of other beings.

The Soul is Brahman, the Eternal.

It is made of consciousness and mind: it is made of life and vision. It is made of the earth and the waters: it is made of air and space. It is made of light and darkness: it is made of desire and peace. It is made of anger and love: it is made of virtue and vice. It is made of all that is near: it is made of all that is afar. It is made of all.

KARMA

According as a man acts and walks in the path of life, so he becomes. He that does good becomes good; he that does evil becomes evil. By pure actions he becomes pure; by evil actions he becomes evil.

And they say in truth that a man is made of desire. As his desire is, so is his faith. As his faith is, so are his works. As his works are, so he becomes. It was said in this verse:

A man comes with his actions to the end of his determination.

Reaching the end of the journey begun by his works on earth, from that world a man returns to this world of human action.

Thus far for the man who lives under desire.

LIBERATION

Now as to the man who is free from desire.

He who is free from desire, whose desire finds fulfilment, since the Spirit is his desire, the powers of life leave him not. He becomes one with Brahman, the Spirit, and enters into the Spirit. There is a verse that says:

When all desires that cling to the heart disappear, then a mortal becomes immortal, and even in this life attains Liberation.

As the slough of a snake lies dead upon an ant-hill, even so the mortal body; but the incorporeal immortal Spirit is life and light and Eternity.

Concerning this are these verses:

I have found the small path known of old that stretches far

away. By it the sages who know the Spirit arise to the regions of heaven and thence beyond to liberation.

It is adorned with white and blue, yellow and green and red. This is the path of the seers of Brahman, of those whose actions are pure and who have inner fire and light.

Into deep darkness fall those who follow action. Into deeper darkness fall those who follow knowledge.

There are worlds of no joy, regions of utter darkness. To those worlds go after death those who in their unwisdom have not wakened up to light.

When awake to the vision of the Atman, our own Self, when a man in truth can say: 'I am He', what desires could lead him to grieve in fever for the body?

He who in the mystery of life has found the Atman, the Spirit, and has awakened to his light, to him as creator belongs the world of the Spirit, for he is this world.

While we are here in this life we may reach the light of wisdom; and if we reach it not, how deep is the darkness. Those who see the light enter life eternal: those who live in darkness enter into sorrow.

When a man sees the Atman, the Self in him, God himself, the Lord of what was and of what shall be, he fears no more.

Before whom the years roll and all the days of the years, him the gods adore as the Light of all lights, as Life immortal;

In whom the five hosts of beings rest and the vastness of space, him I know as Atman immortal, him I know as eternal Brahman.

Those who know him who is the eye of the eye, the ear of the ear, the mind of the mind and the life of life, they know Brahman from the beginning of time.

Even by the mind this truth must be seen: there are not many but only One. Who sees variety and not the Unity wanders on from death to death.

Behold then as One the infinite and eternal One who is in radiance beyond space, the everlasting Soul never born.

Knowing this, let the lover of Brahman follow wisdom. Let him not ponder on many words, for many words are weariness.

Yajñavalkya went on:

This is the great Atman, the Spirit never born, the consciousness of life. He dwells in our own hearts as ruler of all, master of all, lord of all. His greatness becomes not greater by good actions nor less great by evil actions. He is the Lord supreme, sovereign and protector of all beings, the bridge that keeps the worlds apart that they fall not into confusion.

The lovers of Brahman seek him through the sacred *Vedas*, through holy sacrifices, charity, penance and abstinence. He who knows him becomes a Muni, a sage. Pilgrims follow their life of wandering in their longing for his kingdom.

Knowing this, the sages of old desired not offspring. 'What shall we do with offspring,' said they, 'we who possess the Spirit, the whole world?' Rising above the desire of sons, wealth, and the world they followed the life of the pilgrim. For the desire of sons and wealth is the desire of the world. And this desire is vanity.

But the Spirit is not this, is not this. He is incomprehensible, for he cannot be comprehended. He is imperishable, for he cannot pass away. He has no bonds of attachment, for he is free; and free from all bonds he is beyond suffering and fear.

A man who knows this is not moved by grief or exultation on account of the evil or good he has done. He goes beyond both. What is done or left undone grieves him not.

This was said in this sacred verse:

The everlasting greatness of the seer of Brahman is not greater or less great by actions. Let man find the path of the Spirit: who has found this path becomes free from the bonds of evil.

Who knows this and has found peace, he is the lord of himself, his is a calm endurance, and calm concentration. In himself he sees the Spirit, and he sees the Spirit as all.

He is not moved by evil: he removes evil. He is not burned by sin: he burns all sin. And he goes beyond evil, beyond passion, and beyond doubts, for he sees the Eternal.

This is the world of the Spirit, O king. Thus spoke Yajñavalkya.

O Master. Yours is my kingdom and I am yours, said then the king of Videha.

EPILOGUE

THIS is the great never-born Spirit of man, enjoyer of the food of life, and giver of treasure. He finds this treasure who knows this.

This is the great never-born Spirit of man, never old and immortal. This is the Spirit of the universe, a refuge from all fear.   *Brihad. Up. 4. 3-4*

FOR THE BEST IN PAPERBACKS, LOOK FOR THE 🐧

In every corner of the world, on every subject under the sun, Penguin represents quality and variety – the very best in publishing today.

For complete information about books available from Penguin – including Puffins, Penguin Classics and Arkana – and how to order them, write to us at the appropriate address below. Please note that for copyright reasons the selection of books varies from country to country.

In the United Kingdom: Please write to *Dept E.P., Penguin Books Ltd, Harmondsworth, Middlesex, UB7 0DA.*

If you have any difficulty in obtaining a title, please send your order with the correct money, plus ten per cent for postage and packaging, to *PO Box No 11, West Drayton, Middlesex*

In the United States: Please write to *Dept BA, Penguin, 299 Murray Hill Parkway, East Rutherford, New Jersey 07073*

In Canada: Please write to *Penguin Books Canada Ltd, 2801 John Street, Markham, Ontario L3R 1B4*

In Australia: Please write to the *Marketing Department, Penguin Books Australia Ltd, P.O. Box 257, Ringwood, Victoria 3134*

In New Zealand: Please write to the *Marketing Department, Penguin Books (NZ) Ltd, Private Bag, Takapuna, Auckland 9*

In India: Please write to *Penguin Overseas Ltd, 706 Eros Apartments, 56 Nehru Place, New Delhi, 110019*

In the Netherlands: Please write to *Penguin Books Netherlands B.V., Postbus 195, NL–1380AD Weesp*

In West Germany: Please write to *Penguin Books Ltd, Friedrichstrasse 10–12, D–6000 Frankfurt/Main 1*

In Spain: Please write to *Longman Penguin España, Calle San Nicolas 15, E–28013 Madrid*

In Italy: Please write to *Penguin Italia s.r.l., Via Como 4, I-20096 Pioltello (Milano)*

In France: Please write to *Penguin Books Ltd, 39 Rue de Montmorency, F-75003 Paris*

In Japan: Please write to *Longman Penguin Japan Co Ltd, Yamaguchi Building, 2–12–9 Kanda Jimbocho, Chiyoda-Ku, Tokyo 101*